WOODCARVING
TECHNIQUES

Woodcarving Techniques

Rod Naylor

B T BATSFORD LIMITED · LONDON

© Rod Naylor 1979
First published 1979
ISBN 0 7134 0995 9

Filmset by Servis Filmsetting Limited
Manchester
Printed in Great Britain by
The Anchor Press Limited
Tiptree, Essex
for the publishers
B T Batsford Limited
4 Fitzhardinge Street
London W1H 0AH

Contents

Acknowledgment

A special thank you is due to Ron Brown, without whose help I may never have started in business. P R Dicks for photographs 6, 12, 13, 33, 34, 46, 48, 59, 63, 69, 70, 85, 89, 90, 91, 95, 101, 104, 110, 112, 116, 126, 127, 130, 140, 142, and all the other people, too numerous to mention, who have helped in many ways, but particularly my wife who has plied me with coffee and kept our children at bay.

RN **Devizes** 1979

1 Early nineteenth century chair
Satinwood and shellac
By courtesy of The National Trust

Introduction

Modelling and carving are the two main divisions of sculpture. *Modelling* builds up an object from a soft material such as clay. Parts may be added, taken away, pushed, pulled or twisted until the desired shape is reached. *Carving* is the extreme contrast. The artist must see the completed sculpture within the solid block, and then expose it to view. The difficulty is that mistakes must not be made, as more material cannot easily be added.

Sculpture may be described as a form which crystallises an emotion in an onlooker, or a three-dimensional work with an infinite number of viewpoints. It is also the realization of a design without the restriction of the end product having a practical function. As such, the scope for design and originality is infinitely greater in sculptural design than in functional design. However, sculpture and design are closely related; it is merely that one has an aesthetic bias, the other functional.

The basic principles outlined in this book can however be used in other fields of woodwork, for the carving, cabinet making and musical instrument trades are all closely linked. The satinwood chair (1), although delicate, is shaped from substantial volumes of timber, as are many of the stringed musical instruments (2).

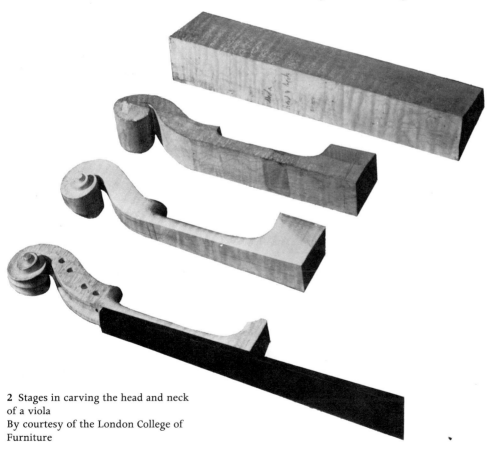

2 Stages in carving the head and neck of a viola
By courtesy of the London College of Furniture

1 Carving and sculpture

3 Detail of carving in a Maori
Meeting House
By courtesy of the High Commissioner
for New Zealand

Origins of sculpture

Twenty thousand years ago, in the caves of the Dordogne in S W France, shapes were accidentally made by dragging hands through the wet clay. This rapidly progressed to making images of animals which the cavemen believed gave them power over the animals represented. This belief is still perpetuated by witches who make images of people and stick pins into them, believing that the living people will suffer corresponding wounds.

Particularly after people became farmers they grew aware of greater and more mysterious powers than the mammoth and bear. An attempt was made to give shape to unknown forces by representing them. This was sometimes achieved by combining the most distinctive human and animal characteristics – sometimes creating a creature of fearsome or awe inspiring appearance (3).

In the same way that earlier sculptors selected certain animal characteristics and combined them to create new creatures, so modern sculptors may select certain features from nature and combine or exaggerate them to create new forms. However, modern forms are not always so readily recognizable (4a, b, c).

4a Gyr falcon. Scraperboard

4b Greek helmets. Scraperboard

4c Knight. Gold plated bronze cast taken from Iroko wood pattern by sand casting process 290mm × 190mm × 225mm (11½in. × 7½in. × 9in.)

The final form depends on the original ideas of the sculptor, the material and the method of shaping it. In the ideal sculpture there is a perfect relationship between the form, material and method of manufacture. New shapes are obtained from new materials or tools. However, what many people refer to as 'modern abstract', is, in parts of the world, very traditional (5).

5 Zulu figure of a man
The Museum of Mankind, London

2 Timber technology

Which wood?

Generally, the harder timbers are more suitable for sculpture. This is because they can often be carved in greater detail, the material is more durable, fire resistant, and a better finish can be obtained. English lime is an exception; though soft it is probably the finest carving timber available as it can even be cut against the grain to some extent. The figuring of the wood grain must also be taken into account, as a bold grain can enhance a simple non-representational form, but completely destroy a portrait.

Hardwoods and softwoods

Wood can be broadly classified into two types – hard and soft. However, this is a biological classification and only bears some relationship to the hardness of the material. Yew, because it is an evergreen with needle-like leaves is classified as soft, though physically it is quite hard. Balsa, with wider leaves which fall in winter is classified as hard, but it is probably the softest and lightest of timbers.

The tree

A tree increases in diameter by adding layers of cells to the outside of the existing timber. The growth rate varies with the climatic conditions, producing a relatively soft layer in spring, and a darker, denser layer of wood in the late summer when growth is slower. These bands of growth are referred to as the annual rings.

When looking at the end of a log it can be divided into three basic parts:

1 *Bark*. This is not normally of any value to the wood carver.
2 *Sapwood*. The sapwood is the living part of the tree and is just under the bark. It is often paler and softer but more prone to attack by woodworm and rot than the heart.
3 *Heartwood*. This is the central, dead supporting part of the tree. It is in all respects the best part of the tree to the sculptor.

Trees normally grow in a slight spiral (6), but the ones to be

6 Timber tends to grow in a slight spiral. Also showing are the sapwood, heartwood and shakes

7 Growth of interlocking grain

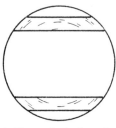

8 These planks have least interlocked grain, but poorest figure

avoided wherever possible are those with interlocked grain, for example, mahogany. Here the wood does not grow straight but in a pronounced spiral. However, as each layer of growth is added to the outside of the tree, the direction of the spiral changes. This produces a wood which cannot easily be cut in the direction of the grain (7).

Flaws

To a greater or lesser extent, all woods have grain, and many have flaws in this, their structure. In traditional carving these flaws are usually a nuisance. However, in non-representational carving, violent twists in the grain and large knots are often very advantageous for they can create movement and vitality. Knots generally radiate from the first annual ring, which may or may not coincide with the centre.

The main hazard in wood is a shake or other form of split, nearly always running along the grain. When a log dries, it loses approximately 25 per cent of its weight and shrinks. Circumferentially, shrinkage is greatest, transversely it is much less, and longitudinally it is barely noticeable. With this knowledge it is possible to calculate how a piece of wood will warp, or even split, as the water dries out or soaks into the wood (9).

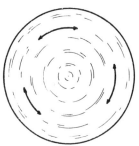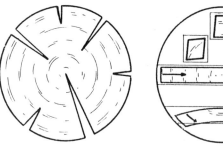

9 Direction of shrinkage

10 Finding a shake

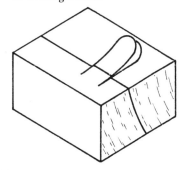

Shakes are not always readily noticeable and there are two easy methods of finding them:

1   By tapping a plank quite hard with a chisel handle. The note often changes when in the vicinity of a shake.

2   By using a gouge to make a groove across a suspected shake, then pulling the gouge away without breaking off the chip. If the end of the chip is gently rubbed it will brake on a shake (10).

Further difficulty arises owing to the fact that a piece of wood is rather like a bundle of very long straws. This causes the wood to dry and shrink quickly at the ends, owing to the open grain, resulting in the material splitting or warping (11). To prevent this happening, a carving block should never be brought directly from a cool damp atmosphere to a warm dry one. It is also preferable

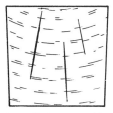

11 Splitting caused by rapid drying

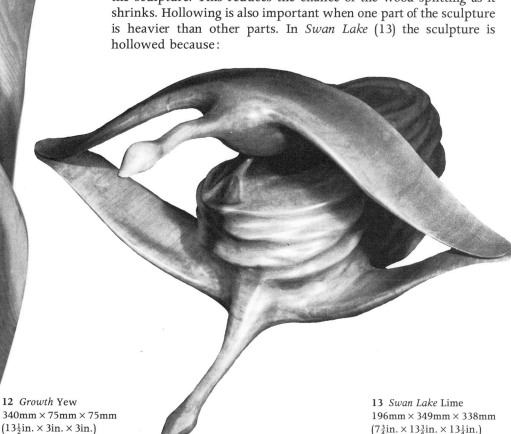

to seal the ends of the wood with glue, paint or thick polish. When a sculpture has been started it is advisable to keep it in a polythene bag until almost ready for polishing.

Further headaches

From illustration 9 we can see that any thick piece of wood which contains the centre of the tree is most prone to splitting. If desperation at being unable to find a block of wood over 75mm (3in.) thick makes it necessary to carve from a round log, then the following could help you to overcome your insanity:

1   Design the sculpture so that no part is very heavy or light in relation to the other parts.

2   Carve very deeply, preferably up to the first annual ring, eg 'growth' (12).

If it is not possible to follow these rules, for example, when sculpting a head, then it is important to keep the work in a polythene bag away from a centrally heated atmosphere, except of course when you are doing the carving. When most of the shaping has been carried out, a large hole should be bored into the bottom of the sculpture. This reduces the chance of the wood splitting as it shrinks. Hollowing is also important when one part of the sculpture is heavier than other parts. In *Swan Lake* (13) the sculpture is hollowed because:

12 *Growth* Yew
340mm × 75mm × 75mm
(13½in. × 3in. × 3in.)
Cellulose and wax

13 *Swan Lake* Lime
196mm × 349mm × 338mm
(7¾in. × 13¾in. × 13¼in.)
Sealer and beeswax

13

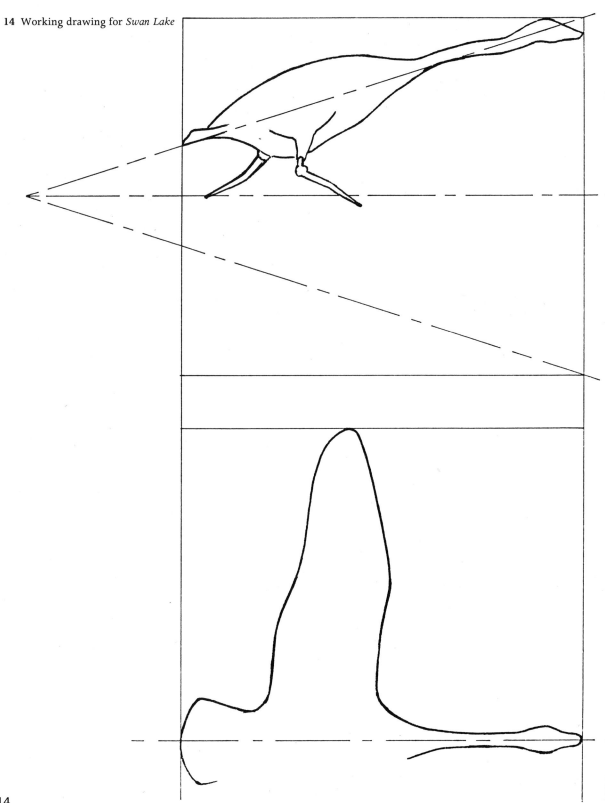

14 Working drawing for *Swan Lake*

1   The weight of the central part could cause the sculpture to break if it were lifted by a wing.
2   Central heating could cause splitting (11).
3   If the sculpture was dropped then the weight of the heavy portion would easily break the lighter parts.

For these reasons the base is hollowed to the point where it is not much thicker than the wings.

Free wood and its seasoning

Wood for sculpture is often available from dead trees in a field or hedge. As a rough guide, the tree should have been dead for one year for every 25mm (1in.) of the tree's diameter, to ensure thorough seasoning. If a live tree is felled, this should be done in the autumn or winter when there is little sap in the wood.

A chain saw, hired for one day, can be used to remove large knots and convert the trunk and branches into logs. Wedges, hammered into the end grain are next used to reduce the logs into suitable blocks. Even if blocks are not required, it is usually important to split the log through the first annual ring to prevent random splitting and reduce weight.

Cutting with wedges is impossible where there is any interlocked grain. In contrast, it is extremely simple with many straight grained timbers. This is particularly true when the wood is riven along the medullary ray – the shiny flecks often seen to radiate from the first annual ring, especially noticeable in oak.

It is at this early stage that some thought should be given to the end product: large carvings cannot be made from small pieces of wood, but a large tree trunk is unmanageable and may not season completely within your working life. Preliminary cuts should be made along any existing large shakes. If, however, the tree trunk is curved, try to retain the hollow side in the largest pieces, as this often provides greater deposits of better quality timber than the opposite side.

Seasoning makes the wood stronger, lighter, more stable and usually more durable. It also improves the ability to take paint and polish. Seasoning is not merely drying, it is the removal of natural sap. In consequence, seasoning can be speeded up by immersing the timber in flowing water. The main direction of shrinkage is around the annual rings (9), radially it is about half of this and lengthwise only 2 to 3 per cent of the shrinkage of the rings. These percentages assume the grain to be straight. Fiddleback and burr figuring have strongly undulating grain, so presenting end grain to all surfaces of the timber and causing the wood to shrink lengthwise.

The degree of seasoning is measured by the moisture content of the wood, and should vary depending on the siting of the finished work. Air-seasoned timber can be as dry as 17 per cent, but kiln-seasoned timber will be approximately 12 per cent, which is much more desirable for centrally heated shops and houses. Owing to this, it is necessary to bring air-dried timber gradually into a centrally heated atmosphere. Moving it straight from the workshop to the mantlepiece directly above the electric fire, could have disasterous results.

Another problem arises when we buy kiln-dried timber in that the wood may be dry when it leaves the kiln. It might then be stored for three months in a muddy yard, during which time the moisture content will steadily rise. Despite the moisture content, kiln-seasoned timber never has quite the same life as air-dried wood.

The basic procedure for artificial seasoning is to stack the timber in the same way as for natural seasoning (16), but in a sealed kiln. The wood is then saturated with steam. Hot air is next circulated. As the humidity is reduced, so is the temperature, until there is only dry air circulating. This cooking process can change the colour, particularly in beech which becomes much darker. The working properties also change, the timber becoming more brittle.

The principle of the artificial seasoning process has certainly been known and used for over a century. Some wood can be seasoned within a few weeks. The seventeenth century method was to immerse the planks in flowing water for up to two years, and then stack the timber for a further ten to twenty years.

Storage

Any wood which has a moisture content just above 20 per cent is prone to fungal attack. As such, timber must not lie on the bare ground but should have air circulating around and through it. There must also be a roof above it and a clean dry floor. The bacteria stained non-representational carving (15), was a happy but rare accident. I have ruined much good timber trying to repeat it. Do not forget to seal any end grain with paint or a similar protective coating, particularly on the harder timbers which are more prone to splitting.

Some species which stain easily, such as sycamore, holly and hornbeam must be brushed clean and stored on end, at least until dry. The storage method for other timbers is to stack the wood horizontally with slats of clean wood between each plank. The strips of wood are placed directly above each other so as to prevent any tendency to sagging and allow adequate ventilation (16).

Timbers

The same design, carved in two different materials will produce two different results. Select a wood sympathetic to the size, shape and design of the finished sculpture, and the place where it will be sited. Weights where shown are the approximate seasoned weight. The first figure is Kg per m3, the second is lb per cu ft.

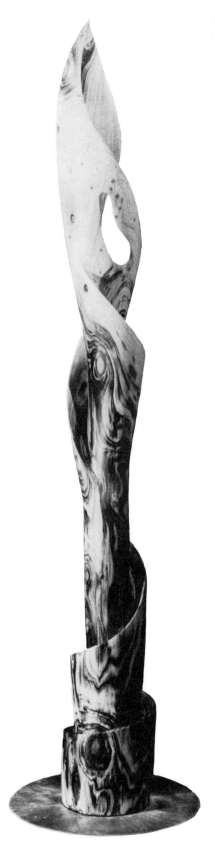

15 *Pillar of Life*
Bacteria stained cyprus fir
495mm × 60mm × 60mm
(19½in. × 2½in. × 2½in.)
Oil and wax

Agba 515 32 Stable, resistant to decay and available in large sizes. Colour varies from yellowish pink to reddish brown. Grain too soft and open for fine detail.

Amboyna Highly figured burr of padauk.

Apple 720 45 Very pale, hard and close grained. Traditionally used for moving parts such as cogs. Only available in small sizes.

Ash, European 690 43 A straight grained nearly white wood. Ideal for bent work and resistance to shock which makes it difficult to use for normal decorative carving. Available in large sizes (93).

Ash, American Similar to European, but often considered inferior. Much easier to work.

Balsa 2½–20 37–320 Wide variation in weight, lighter grades being too soft and spongy. Sometimes used for preliminary models and children's work. Nearly white.

Beech, European 670 42 Light brown to brownish red, but rather plain except for the fine flecks of the medullary ray. Straight grain and fine even texture. Hard but not very stable or durable. Takes detail and is good for making tools. Too difficult for hand working relative to the quality of the end product. Darker wood with wide, well defined annual rings is the hardest and strongest (31).

Box 910 57 Extremely hard and close grained wood with a pale cream colour. Only available in small sizes, but takes exceptionally fine detail (110a, b and 125).

Cedar, Western Red 390 24 A light weight softwood of exceptional durability. Pale yellowish brown turning grey on exposure.

Cherry, European 640 40 Hard and close grained, this pale pinkish brown fruitwood carves well and takes an excellent polish. Only available in small sizes. Darkens with age to a honey colour. American cherry has a redder tint (131).

Chestnut, Spanish or Sweet 545 34 Very similar in appearance and properties to oak, but lacks the medullary ray and is lighter in weight.

Ebony 1,220 76 Very hard, heavy and close grained. Polishes well. Different species vary in colour from pale brown with grey and black streaks through to black. Often simulated by staining pear.

Elm, common English 560 35 Interlocked grain and tendency to warp. Not easy to work but available in large sizes. Durable in very wet situations such as fountains and boats (32).

Elm, rock A tough, dense, strong and durable North American wood. Also used in wet situations.

16 Wood stacks are protected from rain and built on a clean dry surface

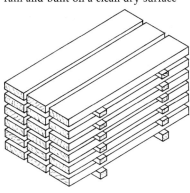

17 Sources of timbers

BIRCH
CEDAR
FIR, DOUGLAS
PINE, YELLOW

HICKORY
OAK
WALNUT, BLACK

BIRCH
CEDAR
MAPLE
FIR, DOUGLAS
PINE, YELLOW
SEQUOIA

BALSA
BOX
CEDAR
GREENHEART
MAHOGANY
ROSEWOOD

MAHOGANY
SATINWOOD

GREENHEART

BALSA
GREENHEART
LANCEWOOD
TULIPWOOD

ASH
BEECH
CHESTNUT, SPANISH
ELM
FIR, DOUGLAS
LARCH
LIME
OAK
PEAR
PLANE
SYCAMORE
YEW

LARCH
PINE
PLANE
SYCAMORE

PINE

CAMPHOR

OAK

TEAK
PADOUK

MAHOGANY
MAPLE
OAK

LAUREL

BLACKWOOD
ROSEWOOD

SATINWOOD

BEECH
BLACK BEAN
CEDAR
OAK

EBONY
MAHOGANY

IROKO
MAHOGANY

BEECH, CAPE
BOX, CAPE

Elm, Wych, Mountain or Scotch 610 38   A British timber, the grain of which is straighter, more finely textured, lighter in colour and rather harder than other elms.

Fir, Douglas, Columbian pine or Oregon pine 530 33   Available in very large sizes and usually with very straight grain. Rather redder than pine. Highly water resistant.

Greenheart 1,040 65   Exceptional strength and durability, especially in sea water. Close straight grain almost free from defects. This wood takes an excellent polish and is suitable for bold simple forms. Splinters from this timber are slightly poisonous. Like other very hard timbers, it is prone to splitting in central heating (104 and 109).

Holly 720 45   White, hard, close, uniform grain and capable of a fine polish. It stains well and was often coloured for decorative furniture. Its hardness makes it very prone to splitting during seasoning. Cutting immediately after felling helps to alleviate this.

Hornbeam 750 47   This very pale wood is hard, strong, tough and resistant to shock. Difficult to carve but turns well and takes a smooth finish. Good for detailed work and small mechanical parts, but not stable or durable.

Horse Chestnut   Creamy white with a fine uniform texture. Not durable or strong.

Iroko 660 41   Similar properties to oak but with interlocked grain. Colour varies from light to dark brown. Not a good carving timber but available in large sizes (38).

Larch 560 35   A strong durable softwood used in boats and outdoor work. Reddish brown heartwood.

Lignum Vitae 1,216 76   One of the hardest and heaviest of timbers. Sapwood is yellowish, heartwood a dark brown and the grain is interlocked. Commonly used for the best carver's mallet heads. Only available in small sizes.

Lime, European 610 38   Creamy white in colour, this wood is straight and close grained yet soft and difficult to split. It is one of the finest carving timbers available, but is unsuitable for external work. Available in large sizes (13 and 98).

Mahogany   See 'Timbers in restoration', page 109.

Oak, American White 720 45   A North American oak which is similar to European in appearance and properties, but subject to variation in quality. Generally inferior to European but imported to England during the mid nineteenth century.

Oak, brown   This is European oak which has a much richer and darker colour. Thought to be due to some slow form of decay.

Oak, European 720 45   The supreme oak for strength and durability. Grain is coarse which makes this unsuitable for very fine work but used almost exclusively in churches. Easily riven along the pronounced medullary ray which appears as shiny markings. Colour normally a pale brown (123 and 124).

Oak, Japanese 670 42   Straight grained and lacking in figure, but softer, lighter and more easily worked than European. Not recommended for external use.

Obeche or African Whitewood 390 24   Soft timber with a pale straw colour which, because of its stability and availability in large sizes, is often used for large works. Internal use only.

Padauk, Andaman 865 54   A dark and distinctive timber, it is strong, durable, hard wearing and available in large sizes. Grain often interlocked.

Padauk, Burma 865 54   Yellowish red to brick red. Too open in grain for very delicate work. Carves well though hard. Durable.

Pear 720 45   Not durable or available in large sizes but cuts well in all directions of the grain which is firm and even. Natural pear has a pale but variable colour, after artificial seasoning it becomes a more uniform pinkish brown (6 and 118).

Pine, pitch 655 41   Relative to other Pines, this is strong, hard and heavy. Yellowish brown, very durable and highly resinous. Formerly popular for church furniture (129).

Pine, sugar 435 27   Similar to Yellow Pine but slightly stronger, harder and obtainable in larger sizes. Pale yellowish white. Used for pattern making.

Pine, yellow, white or Weymouth 438 26   Yellowish white, fine textured, straight grained and easily worked in all directions of the grain. Less shrinkage and warping than most softwoods.

Plane 640 40   Pale yellow to pale red. When cut on the quarter it is called *lace wood* (117).

Rosewood, various species 880 55   A highly decorative wood, usually a rich brown with darker brown or black markings. Very hard but can be split easily along the grain. Unsuitable for fine detail (132).

Sequoia or Californian redwood 470 29   A light weight, pinkish red softwood of exceptional durability. Available in large sizes.

Sycamore 610 38   Creamy white timber with a lustrous fine texture. Carves well and takes detail. As it is odourless and tasteless it is mainly used for kitchen ware. Sometimes used to simulate satinwood, when dyed grey it is called harewood. A member of the maple family (90 and 126).

Teak 720 45   Mid brown timber with an oily nature which makes it very durable but difficult to glue. Works well but too coarse to take fine detail (34).

Walnut, African 540 34   Actually a member of the mahogany family. Golden brown colour without too much interlocked grain, but rather soft. Available in large sizes.

Walnut, American black 640 40   Purplish or greyish brown. Carves in a similar way to European walnut, but much more resistant to decay. Figuring tends to be more dull and uniform (68).

Walnut, European 640 40   Brown, strong and tough, making it very difficult to split. Often highly figured and works well. Prone to attack by woodworm and often very faulty (69 and 133).

Yew 670 42   Hard, exceptionally durable and slow growing soft-wood. Yellowish or reddish brown colour and variegated appearance, particularly near the root. Difficult to work owing to its elasticity and toughness and often has many flaws. Distinctive appearance and polishes extremely well. Traditionally used for the long bow (12 and 134).

Preservation

Woodworm, death watch beetle and some other insects live in timber during the grub stage of their development, and seem to regard many species of timber as great delicacies. The grub stage lasts approximately three years in the common furniture beetle, during which time the grub eats the sound timber and excretes dust. In Spring near the end of the life cycle, the grub changes into a beetle. It then bites its way out of the wood leaving a clean, neat round hole and a trickle of dust. The beetles then immediately mate to begin the life cycle again, twenty to forty eggs being laid in any suitable rough areas of wood.

The furniture beetle is the most common problem and lives in hardwood or softwood, leaving an exit hole approximately 1·5mm ($\frac{1}{16}$in.) diameter (58).

The death watch beetle normally lives in old hardwoods, has a grub stage of about five years and leaves a hole of approximately 3mm ($\frac{1}{8}$in.). This is the thing which goes bump in the night – this distinct noise is the mating call and is made by the insect tapping its head against the wood.

Rot becomes a problem when the moisture content of the wood rises above 20 per cent. Linenfold panelling was often used to cover damp walls while the furniture steadily lowered as the carved feet crumbled on the stone floor. There are many species of fungi, but these are normally broadly classified as *dry rot* and *wet rot*.

True dry rot is the most efficient fungus and can rapidly run rampant through a building. It is recognizable as a fluffy white mass, often with yellow patches. As the fungi develops the wood appears to be coated with a dirty grey plate of matted strands, often tinged with yellow or lilac. Later still it appears as thin branching grey strands. At maturity, the fruit bodies are produced. These pancake like structures have brick red centres with white edges tinged with lilac. The wood becomes dry and brittle after attack, being deeply cracked across the grain into brick shaped pieces. The colour is generally light brown.

Dry rot is more serious and difficult to eradicate than any other fungus. The wood carver must not at this stage attempt to replace the crumbling carving, but should instead call in a specialist to eradicate the trouble.

Wet rot is much more common and is not nearly so serious. There is often no visible fungal growth although it may show as one of many forms; often as black strands or white fluff. The wood is usually very soft and crumbles easily. It may also crack as it dries.

Preservatives, rot killers and woodworm killers are invaluable, and I use the range produced by Cuprinol. These preservatives may be applied by brush, spray or preferably dipping. The dipping time varies with the wood and the degree of protection required – five minutes is usually satisfactory, but some woods can be safely left for a day. If the work is unpolished, dry and warm, then this considerably aids the impregnation which is mainly through the end grain. If brush or spray is used then the liquid should be flooded onto the wood in several coats, until absorption ceases. With very large pieces of timber which cannot be dipped, it is advisable to bore a large hole deeply into the base of the work. This cavity can then be filled with fluid and left, preferably over several weeks to allow penetration. The hole should then be plugged with an offcut from the original carving block. (See Restoration Section.)

Polishing is not normally recommended until the wood has thoroughly dried out. With thin flat panels it is often possible to polish the front of the work, and then apply preservative to the back. Cuprinol, having good penetrative properties, is able to pass through many timbers. Notable exceptions are teak, oak and pitch pine. However, these are so durable that preservatives and killers are rarely needed.

The completed work must never be sited directly on the ground, but must be on a waterproof plinth, or have a plinth with a waterproof membrane under it.

The specific types of Cuprinol important to the wood carver are:

Woodworm Killer. This eradicates all types of beetle as the fluid contains stomach, contact and respiratory insecticides. *Woodworm Killer* also contains a preservative, so preventing reinfestation.

Dry Rot Killer for Timber. This kills dry and wet rots and prevents reinfestation.

5 *Star Wood Treatment.* Kills woodworm, dry rot and wet rot. Reinfestation is also prevented.

Wood Preserver Clear is used in the preservation of sound timber against fungal decay and insect attack.

3 Workshop and tools

Workshop arrangement

The theory sounds fine, but we end up with what we can get. However, try hoping for a spacious ground floor room with good heat and sound insulation, plenty of windows and flexibly controlled fluorescent lighting. It is preferable if the air is not particularly hot, dry or humid. Floors should be solid concrete and perfectly level to the nearest point where a lorry can park.

To enable heavy materials and equipment to be moved it is necessary to have a substantial trolly, approximately 900mm × 600mm (36in. × 24in.) fitted with large castors. To enable you to find your materials and equipment keep them in second hand filing cabinets. Edge tools should be kept in wooden or wood lined drawers. For very large work, an adjustable mirror on castors can be used to increase the efficiency of lighting and optically double the size of your workshop. (Call it a studio if applying for planning permission.) The mirror also saves a great deal of time as it enables assessment of the work from a distance, with only a turn of the head.

The workbench must have a substantial top, preferably a hardwood such as beech, and have a height between 100mm to 125mm (4in. to 5in.) below the carver's elbow. In addition to the large bench, a carver's stand is useful for large figure work, as it enables the work to be seen easily from all angles. This stand has a substantial top with a central hole to take a bench screw.

Sharpening tools

This information is readily available in any woodwork textbook – read several – each will give a different method for moving the tool over the oilstone. Now invent your own. The important thing is to wear the oilstone evenly.

The sharpening angle can, like the sharpening technique, be varied. I grind my larger gouges for rough working at approximately 25° and sharpen at 30°. For delicate finishing work I reduce these angles by up to 10°.

Another area which causes problems is in the use of the leather strop. The leather, when coated with grinding paste does produce a polished finish to the cutting edge. Unfortunately, some tools are made from inferior steel which will cut better and longer if only a medium grade oilstone is used. Under a microscope, the oilstone sharpened cutting edge has the crude efficiency of a bread knife. A beautifully polished cutting edge will blunt much more quickly if the steel is not of the finest quality. The best thing is of course to replace the faulty tool and then use the strop; but rarely does anyone ever take this piece of advice.

Modifying new tools

New tools often need modifying before use:
1   Re-grind gouges to enable arcs to be cut in a smooth flowing curve (18).

18

REMOVE

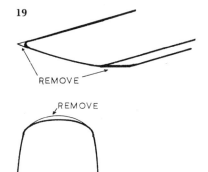

19

REMOVE

REMOVE

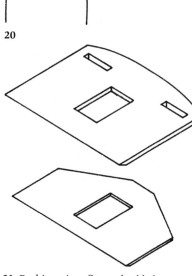

20

21 Packing piece fits under blade

2   Radius the corners of shallow gouges to prevent them digging in, unless the tools are to be used for cleaning up in corners (19). *Note*   If you use an electric grinding wheel, keep dipping the tool in water. If the steel becomes hot it will soften. Emery cloth glued to a piece of wood is quite satisfactory for removing small amounts of steel.

3   Slightly flatten the ends of handles when the tool is to be used for heavy work. This reduces damage to the mallet (20).

4   Spokeshaves are normally designed for general usage, but for quality work with hardwoods a smaller throat is advantageous. To narrow this gap use a sheet of thin metal (an opened out tin can) to make a packing piece which fits behind the blade (21).

Holding the work

Always use a scrap piece of soft wood or thick leather between the carving and any form of clamp.

1   Deep throat G cramps (22).

22 Deep throat G cramp

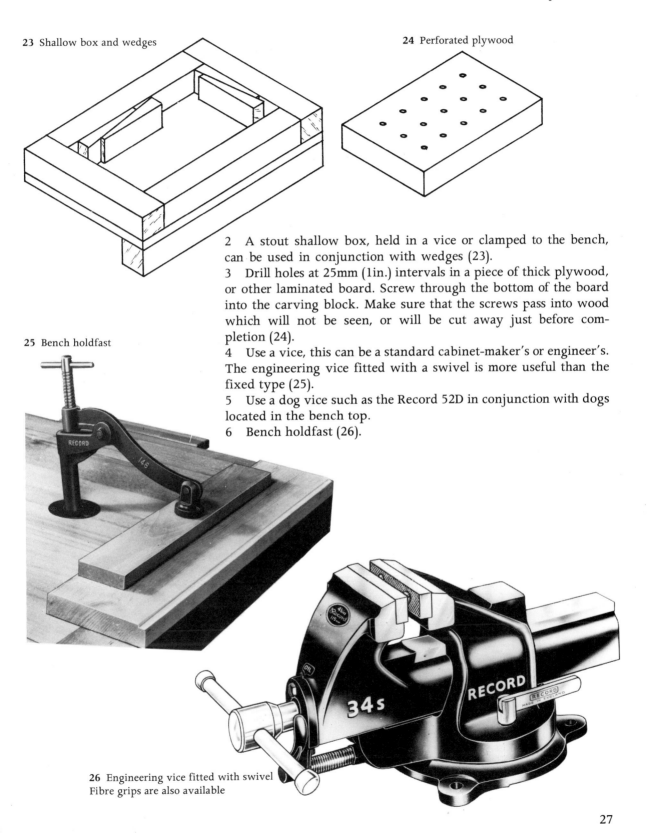

23 Shallow box and wedges

24 Perforated plywood

25 Bench holdfast

2 A stout shallow box, held in a vice or clamped to the bench, can be used in conjunction with wedges (23).

3 Drill holes at 25mm (1in.) intervals in a piece of thick plywood, or other laminated board. Screw through the bottom of the board into the carving block. Make sure that the screws pass into wood which will not be seen, or will be cut away just before completion (24).

4 Use a vice, this can be a standard cabinet-maker's or engineer's. The engineering vice fitted with a swivel is more useful than the fixed type (25).

5 Use a dog vice such as the Record 52D in conjunction with dogs located in the bench top.

6 Bench holdfast (26).

26 Engineering vice fitted with swivel Fibre grips are also available

27 Carvers' screw

7   Carver's bench screw. If it is not practical to have a large hole in the bottom of the work, it can be glued to a piece of waste wood with several layers of newspaper between (27). If a water soluble glue is used, it can be later dissolved (27).

8   Carver's chops.

9   Buttons (28).

10   Jet clamps. These are very useful as they have the luxury of interchangeable face pads (29).

28 Buttons

29 Jet clamp

Holding the tools

Most people understand the basic principle of holding the carving tools firmly with one hand while using the mallet with the other. This is most satisfactory except for delicate finishing work, for which I grip the handle with one hand to provide the forward pressure, also placing my shoulder or chest against it if necessary. My other hand holds the blade, so guiding the tool and at the same time pulling it backwards. It is the combination of these opposing forces which I consider to give greater accuracy in many instances.

30 Lip and spur drill

RIDGWAY

Drilling

Drilling may be used to make individual holes or, by making the holes overlap, cut up the timber. The latter is particularly useful for enclosed areas where a saw cannot reach and when the timber is too large or heavy for the bandsaw. Also, the drill is very efficient for lowering the ground on a low relief.

Rough holes made to speed up the carving may be drilled with a brace and Jennings' pattern auger bit. Alternatively an electric drill fitted with a Ridgway flatbit is one of the cheapest and most efficient tools for this. Used in even a small electric drill it will cut quickly and, in conjunction with extension shanks it will bore to any depth.

For cutting a block of wood to shape when a bandsaw is not available I adopt the following method:

1 Small pieces of wood to be placed on the drill stand should have both top and bottom planed flat and parallel. Large baulks of timber must have one surface planed flat. I then use an ordinary electric hand drill fitted to a bench stand, which I heavily weight with lead. The stand is then placed directly onto the timber, but with the drill twisted around so that it is not above the table.

2 Use carbon paper to copy the design onto the wood.

3 A saw tooth machine centre bit (R542) can be used for large holes or a lip and spur drill (30), for small holes. The idea is to drill a hole which slightly overlaps the previous hole and just touches the outline of the design. Bits fitted to a brace and many other types of machine held bit are not designed for this type of work and will either drift into the adjacent hole or tear out the fibres of the wood, so entailing a lot of extra time spent on finishing.

4 With fully three dimensional work for which I have worked out detailed drawings of both front and side views I omit some of the holes in stage three, so that the complete block is still held together. One side of the timber must also be flat and square to the face. Copy the side view onto the second prepared surface, using a trysquare to ensure that it is perfectly level with the first drawing. Drill around this second drawing and complete any drilling omitted in the third stage.

The sculpture has now attained the basic shape which can probably be best completed by hand methods.

Industrial machines are generally useful, but try not to be tempted into designing a work for ease of production. Once you start doing that you might as well make it in plastic.

Sawing

Saws which are of any value to the woodcarver can be broadly classified into several basic types:

1 *Chain saws.* Not economically viable except to the larger companies. It is much more realistic to hire one for any large jobs.

2 *Log saws.* Cheap saws are generally hard work – an inferior

log saw will also guarantee that your knuckles are skinned after only minutes of use. Use a saw, the handgrip of which is fitted with a guard.

3   *Handsaws* can be sub-divided into cross-cut and rip. *Rip saws* have large teeth which cut like chisels. They can only be used for cutting along the grain and should be held at 60° to the wood. *Cross-cut saws* have smaller teeth which are rather like knives and are most efficient when held at 45° for cutting across the grain. They can, however, also cut along the grain. Handsaws are made in a wide variety of grades, but the only ones worth considering are those with a taper ground blade. Select one with fine teeth for cutting dry hardwoods, slightly larger teeth for softwoods.

4   *Backsaws* have a very thin blade with fine teeth to allow precision workmanship. As these blades are so delicate they are, in the best saws stiffened with a heavy brass back – lesser saws have a steel back. Backsaws can again be sub-divided into two types – tenon and dovetail. Tenon saws are the ones usually used for precision work. The dovetail saw is similar to the tenon saw, but has a smaller and thinner blade with much finer teeth. Dovetail saws are the ultimate for the precision sawing of straight lines in wood. These are the backsaws used for making *The Bowler* (112).

5   *Bow saws.* The basic design of a bow saw has remained unchanged for many centuries. Earlier ones may have had wide blades so making them more accurate for cutting straight lines, or narrow blades for shaped work. Fitted with a narrow blade, the M2400 twine strained bow saw is ideal for shaped work. It is also suitable for antique restoration as it copies the old tool markings. Another advantage of the bow saw is that the thin blade can be passed through a previously drilled hole, so making it ideal for pierced work (31 and 32).

31 Bow saw

32 Dunster Castle. Pierced and carved
elm panel and carved oak mouldings
c 1680. When originally made, this
carving was painted a stone colour
with silvered highlights
By courtesy of The National Trust

Adhesives

In a well glued joint there should be no film of glue. The bonding
of the surfaces is achieved by the knitting together of the glue
soaked fibres of the surfaces. Surplus glue merely impedes this;
which is why the joints must be accurate, the glue should be thin
at the time of using and surplus squeezed out.

A glued joint is strongest when the wood fibres of both pieces
are parallel. Rather weaker is the joint where the fibres of one
piece of wood are at right angles to another. This is because there
is not the same knitting effect and the shrinkages are in different
directions. This usually reduces the strength by at least half and
it may well be less than one quarter of the strength of a similar
joint with parallel fibres. Gluing where one or both surfaces is end
grain is even weaker. As end grain readily absorbs the adhesive
it should be given a preliminary sizing, ie a very thin solution of
glue.

The bonding of two different species of timber can cause
further problems for, as the woods age they will dry and shrink,
but at different rates.

Traditional glues are made by heating the cleaned bones and
skins of animals in water. This produces a glue which can be very
efficient, but has its limitations. The main problems are that the
glue will turn to jelly in damp conditions, but crystallize in central
heating. Some modern adhesives are more efficient than this,
others have even worse problems, for they can be so strong that
subsequent restoration is made extremely difficult.

Although the purist would say that restoration should be carried
out with the original glue, the craftsman can reply that the job
should be carried out efficiently. Even with a reproduction the
same arguments can be made as nearly all genuine antiques have
at some point been restored. Anyway, it is reasonably easy to
give an approximate date to any visible traces of animal glue.

The adhesive which I normally use for gluing wood to wood on works sited indoors is a polyvinyl acetate such as *Evo-Stik* Resin 'W'. This glue is not particularly waterproof or heatproof, making it unsuitable for external use or fireplaces. The liquid glue can also be destroyed by frost. These disadvantages are small when compared to the advantages. PVA is a one part water based glue which at most requires stirring to make it ready for use. It is applied cold and quickly sets at room temperature to provide a very powerful bond. This glue, however, never becomes brittle, so allowing some movement of the timber without breaking the adhesive film. *Evo-Stik* forms a firm bond even without the use of heavy clamps – very useful if you are trying to restore a wooden 'flower'. Even

33 *Vertebrae* Bronze cast from wooden pattern
Lost wax process
137mm × 465mm × 125mm
($5\frac{3}{8}$in. × $18\frac{3}{8}$in. × 5in.)

with large joints, the technique I often use is to stretch strips of masking tape and stick it over the joint. The natural elasticity of the tape is often sufficient, and in many pieces of complex carving it is the only way of holding the pieces of wood together.

PVA is particularly suitable for use on furniture. Chairs and many other pieces of furniture will need restoration every half century. This often means dismantling the parts, which is made much easier if a water-soluble glue was originally used. A hypodermic syringe can be used to inject the water through a very small hole. Sometimes however, damage which could possibly be caused by dismantling the furniture is greater than the advantages of complete restoration. In an instance like this, a hypodermic syringe can also be used to inject the *Evo-Stik* directly into the joint. This is not so efficient as dismantling the pieces for the joints may not fit accurately and will be contaminated by old glue; but it is probably the lesser of the evils.

For external use or fireplace construction, the synthetic resins are extremely efficient. Urea-formaldehyde, such as *Aerolite* 306, is an efficient wood glue. It is highly water resistant, heat resistant and immune to attack by moulds or fungi. This adhesive is widely used in extreme climatic conditions and is also suitable for laminating large blocks of wood, where the completed assembly is to be worked as one piece.

Of more general use are the epoxy resins such as *Araldite* or *Araldite Rapid*. Despite the high cost of these adhesives they are invaluable for bonding impervious materials such as glass and metal, and are one of the few adhesives with gap filling properties. Many glues set by evaporation of a fluid. *Araldite* sets by a chemical reaction, so allowing large quantities to set rapidly without shrinkage. It is suitable for bonding stainless steel or brass rods into stone plinths, fitting ivory or glass eyes into wooden or cast bronze sculptures and almost any job where a permanent bond is required.

Araldite Rapid is most suitable for very small jobs which can be quickly assembled. For larger jobs which cannot be assembled within a few minutes, it is necessary to use *Araldite*. Like all glues, the setting time can vary widely according to temperature.

4 Design and scaling

34 *Fluid vertebrae* Teak
76mm × 400mm × 70mm
(3in. × 15¾in. × 2¾in.)
Teak oil

Principles of design – points to ponder

To understand a carving or sculpture it is important to understand the methods of shaping and the media used. In the ideal form there is a perfect relationship between the form, material and method of manufacture. New shapes are obtained from new materials or tools.

Vertebrae (33) and *Fluid Vertebrae* (34) were both inspired by the same piece of bone from a rabbit's vertebrae. *Fluid Vertebrae* was hand held and shaped with carver's gouges. Apart from preliminary shaping with an adze and some finishing with gouges, *Vertebrae* was made with cabinet maker's tools and techniques. For short flat areas the 3 in 1 plane was invaluable (35). The small curves between the flat areas were made with an inside ground gouge.

Design is the principle of craftsmanship. A day or a week spent designing even a simple piece is more than repaid in the quality of the finished sculpture. Skill with the tools is not enough.

The full power of sculpture is obtained in the third dimension, not a low relief. It should also be different when seen from every position, as a symmetrical mass is using less than half the available number of viewpoints.

35 3 in 1 plane

36 Model staircase. Early nineteenth century. Mahogany
685mm (27in.)
The Victoria and Albert Museum,
London

37 *Amazone* Yew
1m 320mm (4ft. 4in.)
Boiled linseed oil diluted with an
equal volume of white spirit
Zigfrids Sapietis

The depth of carving helps to show the quality of the work. Strong contrasts between high and low will highlight the most important part of the work, or make a carving visible when placed in a diffused north light. In contrast, work to be sited outside in the tropics can be subjected to such strong overhead lighting that virtually no undercutting is necessary.

It is often helpful to ensure that the dimensions are different, for example, width could be five-eighths of the height and thickness five-eighths of the width. These proportions are not of course rigid and I make many sculptures where the height is three times greater than the width. Different parts of the sculpture should also have different sizes, but they must balance. It is probably unwise for the beginner to design a work where one part is extremely thick, thin, large or small, relative to other parts. The unity of a sculpture also applies to the style, which must be in complete unity throughout, and to the colour. The sap wood, apart from its poor physical properties, is often excessively contrasting with the heart. Even the figuring should not normally be excessively bold, unless the sculpture is of a very simple form.

Sculpture should relate to its surroundings – in mountainous country large, strong and solid (37), for the home more delicate

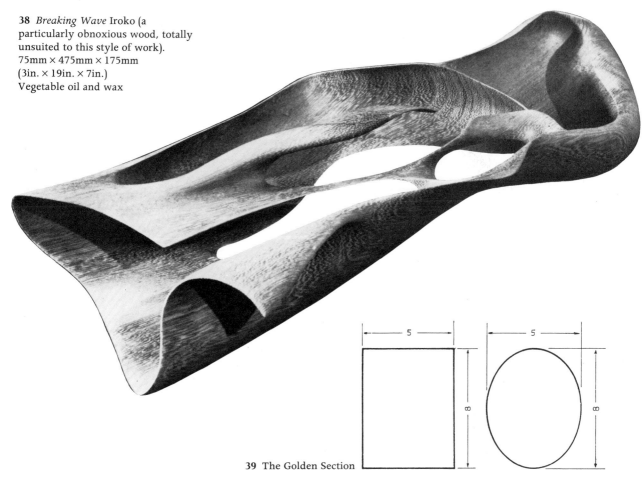

38 *Breaking Wave* Iroko (a particularly obnoxious wood, totally unsuited to this style of work). 75mm × 475mm × 175mm (3in. × 19in. × 7in.) Vegetable oil and wax

39 The Golden Section

subtle and graceful (36). Carving should also relate to its immediate surroundings – a human head fits nicely into an elliptical panel (85), but is seldom quite harmonious with a square one.

The hollow form can be of more interest than the solid, for the hollow form has an inside and an outside, with a consequent increase in surface area and interesting features (38).

A sculpture is not at its best when there is nothing more to add, but when there is nothing more to take away (104).

A sculpture is composed from a series of lines which may be straight, crooked or curved. Straight lines can create boredom or strong and bold forms (4c and 33). Crooked lines are disorganized and ugly. A curved line, containing a variety of subtle shapes can have a rhythm which is interesting and form a sculpture which might be good (34 and 104).

The Golden Section is merely a proportion of 5:8 between the measurements of a rectangle, major and minor axes of an ellipse or other geometric shape (39). These are the proportions which experiments have shown to be the best.

Optical movement can be created by a series of lines or areas of light and shade, which flow through the design (33 and 112).

The optical centre is just above the geometric centre (40). Focal points within a sculpture are usually best if they are on or above the optical centre. Some of the main points of interest within an overall form and the lines within it (41).

40   GEOMETRIC CENTRE   OPTICAL CENTRE

Matching grain pattern to shape

A slim elegant fish, gracefully streamlined as it flashes across your vision. But what happens if the harsh lines of the figuring were to run at right angles to the flow of the form? First, the timber selected should have a fine texture and subtle colouring to blend with the delicate shape of a fish. Second, the timber should be selected, or the work designed, to create a harmony between the overall form and the lines within it (42).

(a) Annual rings nearly parallel to one face produce two surfaces with bold irregular patterns and rapid colour and pattern changes as these are cut away (43).

(b) Annual rings run diagonally across ends. Streamlined grain pattern on all surfaces. Little change in colour or grain as the wood is cut away.

(c) A curve, cut into the timber as shown produces a curved grain pattern.

(d) Cut the opposite surface parallel to the curve.

(e) Cut the upper and lower areas of the block parallel to the figuring. This produces the basic form from which we could carve a slim streamlined fish.

Highly figured timbers are suitable for simple forms, as they need little to decorate them. If however a bold patch of unharmonious figuring is found when the carving is nearing completion, then bleach can be used to fade it into insignificance. Some of the stronger household bleaches will fade some woods. Stronger bleaches are specially prepared for woodworkers and are available from specialist suppliers. See page 118.

41 Main points of interest in a shape

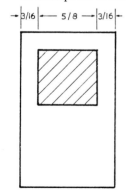
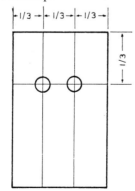
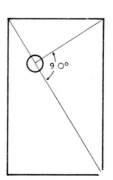
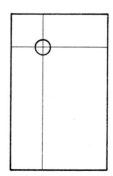

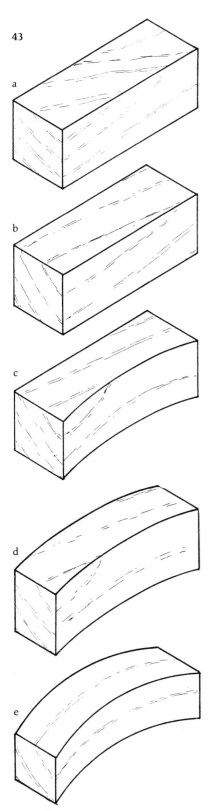

43

a

b

c

d

e

42 *Dolphin* Burmese teak
135mm × 457mm × 108mm
(5¼in. × 18in. × 4¼in.)
Wax
A Mandl

Scaling

After completing the preliminary drawing, it may need scaling up or down to suit the wood. The size must also be harmonious with the future surroundings of the completed carving.

1   Pantograph. This can be easily and cheaply found in many toyshops. The Pantograph can be used to scale up or down, but usually in a fixed and restricting ratio. Some specialist shops also sell more sophisticated pantographs.

2   Squared paper. Also scales up or down and can be used to change the proportions by changing the squares into rectangles.

3   Look at your design in a mirror and draw around the reflection with a felt tip pen. Trace this onto paper and reverse it to right the image.

4   The most accurate method is to take a slide and project this onto the wood or paper. This technique, like number three, is suitable for shortening or elongating designs by putting the drawing at an angle to the mirror or camera. Proportions can also be changed by projecting the slide onto a sheet of paper which is at an angle to the projector.

5   Enlargements are readily made with an episcope, if you are lucky enough to find one.

5 Examples of work

The following examples must not be slavishly copied. Use them as sources of inspiration, but try to create something with your own unique style. In contrast, restoration work demands slavish copying, for every master of every age has tackled the same problem in a slightly different way. This results in Miss World having one set of statistics, and the Venus de Milo another.

Chip carving

Chip carving is an incised geometric decoration which is reasonably uniform over a given area. The main characteristic is the obvious patience required to create the design, the units often being less than 6mm ($\frac{1}{4}$in.) in length.

Over a large area, about two-thirds should be left blank. A small object such as a jewellery box can have a larger proportion of carving. The work is always best carried out in a very fine grained wood without figure, such as pear or sycamore. Despite this it was frequently used to decorate early oak furniture (45).

Chip carving has been used in England since 1300, but became popular about 1525. When trying to copy an old circular design, note that it will no longer be circular. Though accurately marked out with dividers, the wood will have shrunk across the grain. The difference between the two axes will be approximately 5mm ($\frac{3}{16}$in.) for every 300mm (12in.) diameter.

Many of the units can be made in two cuts, the work either being designed to fit the tools, or the tools being ground to fit the design. All the downward stabs are first made to cut the grain and the waste is then removed with the second cut. If a downward cut is made and an adjoining chip has already been removed, then the wedge shape of the blade is liable to break out part of the design.

45 Clamped chest *c* 1300. Oak 508mm × 1m 65mm × 483mm (1ft 8in. × 3ft 6in. × 1ft 7in.) The Victoria and Albert Museum, London

46 and **47** Examples of chip carving
Cherry

48 Crocodile. Teak with chip carved
back and glass eyes
20mm × 178mm × 25mm
($\frac{3}{4}$in. × 7in. × 1in.)

When a knife is used it should have a short blade, and cutting may be towards or away from the body. The knife is held tightly and the cutting action is with the hand, not the arm. Extra pressure may be obtained by using the thumb of the other hand against the back of the blade, but there must be a lot of tension in the hands – it is the tension which gives the accuracy of a braking force combined with a pushing force.

For other examples of chip carving see illustrations 46, 47, 48 and 141.

Carving dishes, eg sandwich tray (49)

Commercially produced woodware is normally designed for ease of production. This restricts the form of the end product and brainwashes us into believing that a given object should have a certain size and shape. The basic restrictions are as follows:

Function

A container for holding sandwiches.

Design factors

1   Size and shape of a sandwich.
2   The number of sandwiches eaten during a meal.
3   Hygiene.
   a   The tray must be washable or polished with something which is, eg teak has natural oils which resist water.
   b   There must not be any sharp corners where germs could breed.
   c   The wood should have small pores to make it smoother, or be polished with something which fills the pores.
4   The material should preferably be odourless and tasteless, or polished with something which is.
5   Aesthetic.
6   When completed, the tray should have an almost constant thickness to reduce the possibility of the wood warping or splitting.
7   Cost.

The above factors can be modified slightly to suit many other items of household woodware (50, 51 and 52).

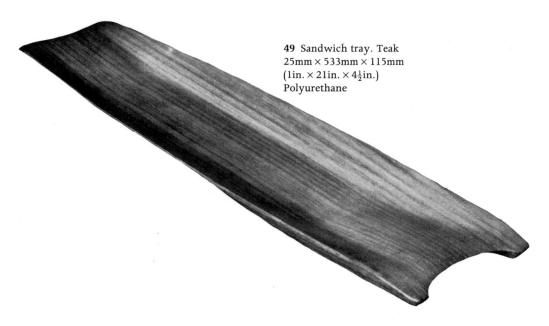

49 Sandwich tray. Teak
25mm × 533mm × 115mm
(1in. × 21in. × 4½in.)
Polyurethane

50 Fruit bowl. Teak
50mm × 394mm × 210mm
(2in. × 15½in. × 8¼in.)
Vegetable oil

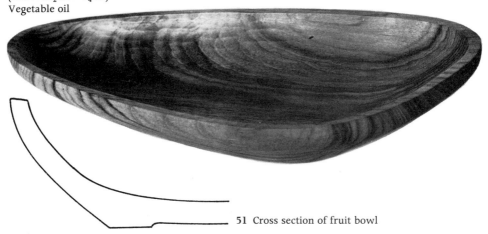

51 Cross section of fruit bowl

52 Meat carving
board. The other
side of the board is
flat to allow for use
as a cheese board
or bread board.
Teak 25mm ×
356mm × 190mm
(1in. × 14in. ×
7½in.)
Vegetable oil

Mouldings

Wooden moulding planes of the late nineteenth and early twentieth centuries are still plentiful, although they were used long before this. However, for working large amounts of material they cannot compete with a spindle moulder or router. For shaping small lengths the wooden moulding plane is efficient, if you can find one with the required cutter.

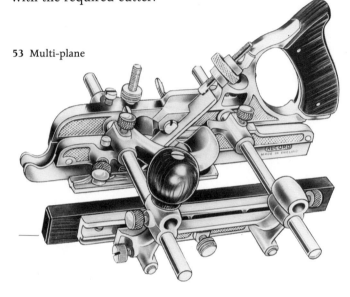

53 Multi-plane

The modern equivalent of the wooden plane is an iron plough, combination or multi plane (53), with the luxury of adjustable fences and a range of interchangeable cutters. The Record multi plane has a total of forty interchangeable cutters, and the option of re-grinding them to cut almost any shape.

Another important moulding tool is the scratch stock, which has been used since the fifteenth century. A scratch stock is advantageous in that it will cut stopped mouldings, follow curves and seldom tears the grain. Also, it can easily be used to make missing pieces for old mouldings or cut forms of unorthodox section. Disadvantages are that the cutter blunts quickly and can only be used to work small sections. The tool consists simply of two L-shaped pieces of wood, usually beech, screwed or bolted together. Between these is the cutter which is an old piece of scraper or saw blade, filed square across to the reverse of the required section (54).

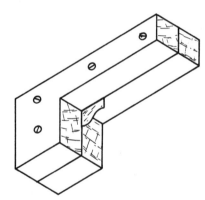

54 Scratch stock

For working mouldings or inlaying on circular wood, such as a table leg, the scratch stock can be used in conjunction with a moulding box (55). Moulding boxes must be stoutly made, so that the circular wood can be held in place with folding wedges. The scratch stock then works against the square edge of the box.

In the corner cupboard (56), the feet were shaped with rebate

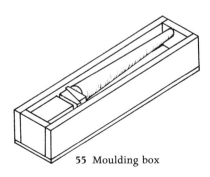

55 Moulding box

and moulding planes and then sawn out. Other mouldings were made with the scratch stock, except for the swan neck pediment. This was made with carving tools and in places finished with a scratch stock. The chair in illustration 57 could also be made by the same combination of scratch stock and carving tools.

Some mouldings which at first sight appear to be carved, were in fact turned on a lathe. A typical example is the curved moulding above the arched dial of a grandfather clock. The wood to be moulded can be glued to a piece of waste wood with soluble glue. After turning the glue is dissolved.

56 Corner cupboard. Mahogany 2m 160mm (7ft 1in.) Shellac and wax

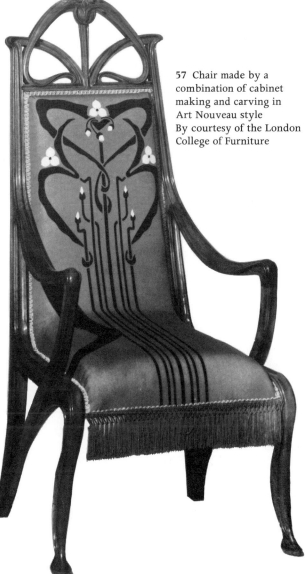

57 Chair made by a combination of cabinet making and carving in Art Nouveau style By courtesy of the London College of Furniture

With the dining table central column of illustration 58, turning was completed to the profile of the left hand side. Carving of the acanthus leaves was then completed by hand.

Other examples of mouldings and carved mouldings can be seen in illustrations 59 and 60.

58 Central column from dining table. Early Victorian. Walnut – turned, carved and eaten by woodworm. Shellac

59 Carved mouldings By courtesy of the Keevil Collection, Camden Works Museum   **60** Cross sections of mouldings

Turning

Primitive lathes have been used in different parts of the world for several thousand years. In England, turning was revived during the early sixteenth century, the pole lathe being used until the early twentieth century. From the early seventeenth century the treadle lathe (62), was also used. Treadle lathes are more efficient than pole lathes and after the mid eighteenth century they could also be used for carrying out twist turning (69). Modern electric lathes are supposed to be a refinement of the treadle lathe.

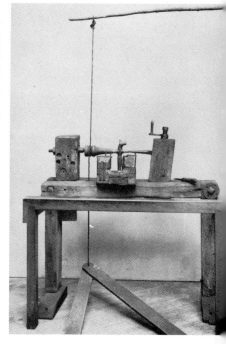

61 Pole lathe
The Science Museum, London

62 Treadle lathe
Author's collection

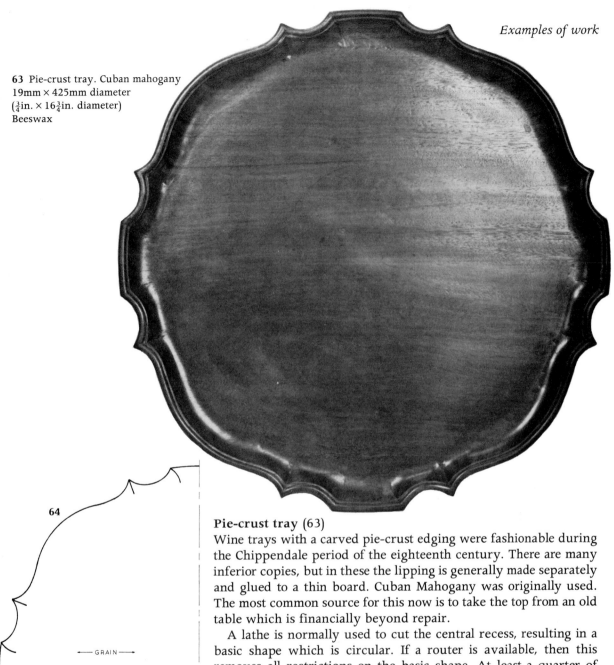

63 Pie-crust tray. Cuban mahogany
19mm × 425mm diameter
($\frac{3}{4}$in. × 16$\frac{3}{4}$in. diameter)
Beeswax

64

← GRAIN →

CROSS–SECTION OF COMPLETED TRAY

TURNED SECTION

CARVING STARTED

NEARING COMPLETION

Pie-crust tray (63)

Wine trays with a carved pie-crust edging were fashionable during the Chippendale period of the eighteenth century. There are many inferior copies, but in these the lipping is generally made separately and glued to a thin board. Cuban Mahogany was originally used. The most common source for this now is to take the top from an old table which is financially beyond repair.

A lathe is normally used to cut the central recess, resulting in a basic shape which is circular. If a router is available, then this removes all restrictions on the basic shape. At least a quarter of the design should be drawn full size, with a cross-section to calculate the limit of the recess which can be turned. When an old tray is to be copied, note that the basic shape will now be an ellipse. This is because an eighteenth century tray will have shrunk across the grain by approximately 5mm ($\frac{3}{16}$in.) for every 300mm (12in.) of diameter. It is thus necessary to leave the edge slightly thicker than necessary, so enabling the basic shape to be carved before starting work on the detail. Choose the grain direction carefully and make sure that there is a good contrast between the sizes of each element in the design of the edge.

49

The basic procedure is:

1   The wood to be turned can be screwed directly to the faceplate. A better method, particularly when copying an antique tray, is to screw some waste wood to the faceplate and glue the turning block to this. Water soluble animal glue should be used, with several layers of newspaper between the blank and the waste wood. When using an antique table top, the lower surface of the top will become the lower surface of the tray, complete with blemishes and antique tool markings. Turn to the section in illustration 64b.

2   Remove the work and carve into a slight ellipse if required. The minor axis of the ellipse must be directly across the grain. When the tray is clamped, a block of scrap wood must be placed inside it to prevent splitting.

3   Mark out the external shape from a template (64a).

4   Saw out the external shape and complete it with a wide gouge and chisel. An authentic Chippendale tray would almost certainly have been sawn with a bow saw (31).

5   The inner side of the beaded edge is now drawn using a finger as a gauge. I prefer to use a 90° V tool and wide shallow gouge to carve up to this line (64c).

6   Mark in the outer line of the hollow and cut it roughly to shape with a wide shallow gouge (64d).

7   Use a pair of compasses to mark the main points at the inside of the hollow, then draw the rest freehand. Level the bottom of the tray up to this inner line (64a).

8   Check illustrations 64a carefully and note the curves and angles between the different segments of the design. Use a gouge to complete the shaping of the hollow as started in stage 6, and a V tool to give crisp corners.

9   If a reproduction tray is being made, read chapter 7.

Other designs for pie-crust trays can be seen in illustration 65.

65 Designs for pie-crust trays

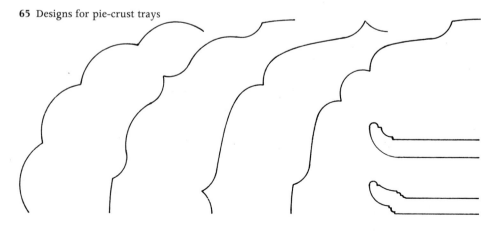

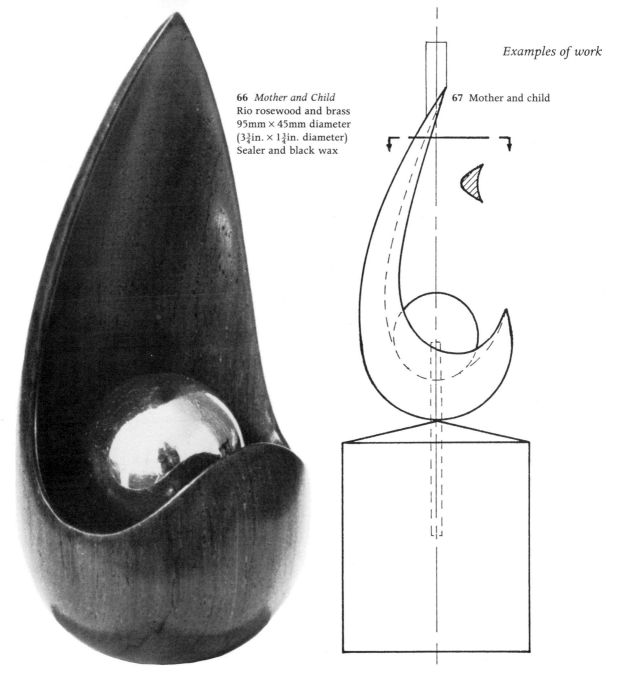

66 *Mother and Child*
Rio rosewood and brass
95mm × 45mm diameter
(3¾in. × 1¾in. diameter)
Sealer and black wax

67 Mother and child

A partially turned sculpture – Mother and Child (66)
This piece of sculpture was turned on a lathe to the shape shown
by the outer line (67). It was then completed by hand carving. The
wood selected was Rio Rosewood, a rich brown material which
contrasts well with the brass. Support is provided by a brass rod
which passes from the centre of the sphere, through the Rosewood
and into the centre of the base.

Another example of combining two different materials is the
sculpture *Sanctuary* (68). This consists of a walnut log, split open
and carved, the polished timber contrasting with an egg shell white
cast stone centrepiece.

68 *Sanctuary* Walnut with cast stone
centrepiece
990mm (39in.)
Ralph R. Baney

70 Double open twist candlestick
c 1850. Walnut
222mm (8¾in.)
Shellac
By courtesy of the Bell-Knight
Collection

69 Seventeenth century style table
with twist turned legs. Walnut
737mm × 840mm × 559mm
(29in. × 33in. × 22in.)
D Wood

Twist turning

Twist turning was commonly used during the walnut period of the late seventeenth and early eighteenth centuries (69). The early hand method was to first complete the turning and then mark out the spiral by winding a piece of paper around the column. A saw cut, made to the required depth of carving, replaces the pencil mark. Forming the spiral is then carried out by hand carving methods.

When a double twist is wanted the marking out process is repeated twice, the second start and finish being exactly opposite the first. Triple twists are made in a similar way. Each twist can be shallowly carved, or cut right into the centre, giving a much more delicate appearance (70).

The lathe which mechanically carried out the Twist Turning process is a mid eighteenth century invention, although not popularized until a century later. Usually, a right hand spiral was used, ie, rising towards the right. Despite this I consider that it looks better when used in pairs of right and left, with the spiral rising away from the opening which it frames.

Further examples of twist turning can be seen in illustration 71.

71 Examples of twist turning

SINGLE
BINE
TWIST

DOUBLE
TWIST

FLUTED
TWIST

FIDDLE
HEAD
TWIST

LATCHEE
TWIST

POINT
TWIST

73 Bedstead end *c* 1545. Oak
1m 260mm (4ft 1½in.)
The Victoria and Albert Museum,
London

Linenfold (73, 74)

Panelling in Britain has been used since approximately AD 1400, but linenfold carving started to become popular a century later. A rebate plane is first used around the edges of the panel to lower the background. Straight hollows are next cut with a moulding plane or a multi plane, only the ends being hand carved.

Further examples of linenfold designs can be seen in illustrations 75–79.

74 Gothic chair with linenfold panels
Late fifteenth century
By courtesy of the Musée des Arts
Décoratifs

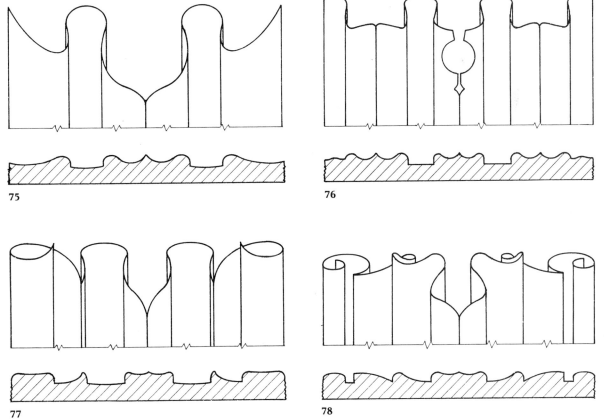

75

76

77

78

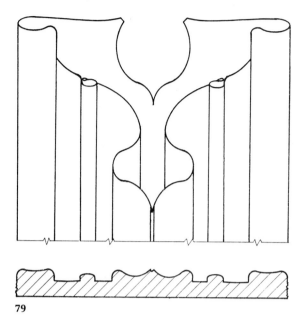

79

Crossbow

Design The Wildcat crossbow shown in illustration 80, was selected for inclusion because the design is efficient, yet provides a springboard for considerable modification and refinement. More detailed drawings and component parts such as the trigger mechanism are also available, so that it is possible to purchase any part which the craftsman cannot manufacture.

A first point to note is the error in the working drawing (81). Quarter sawn timber is the least prone to warping. Consequently, the crossbow will be of greater accuracy if the section is like that illustrated (82).

If the basic design is modified, here are some design principles to bear in mind:

1   Crossbow bolts may be travelling down the stock in excess of 320 km/h (200 mph), which means that the slot must be perfectly accurate and polished. This slot must be of sufficient depth to allow clearance of the bolt feathers.

2   Do not reduce the cross section of the stock at section AA, or dispense with the finger grooves. This would bring your fingers dangerously close to the string.

3   Fit a trigger guard and safety catch.

4   A bow or prod with a draw weight in excess of 46 kg (100 lb) may need some aid to assist cocking. The simplest form of aid is a stirrup through which one or both feet can be placed during cocking. There are of course many other more complex but efficient systems.

80 Wildcat crossbow
B and P Barnett

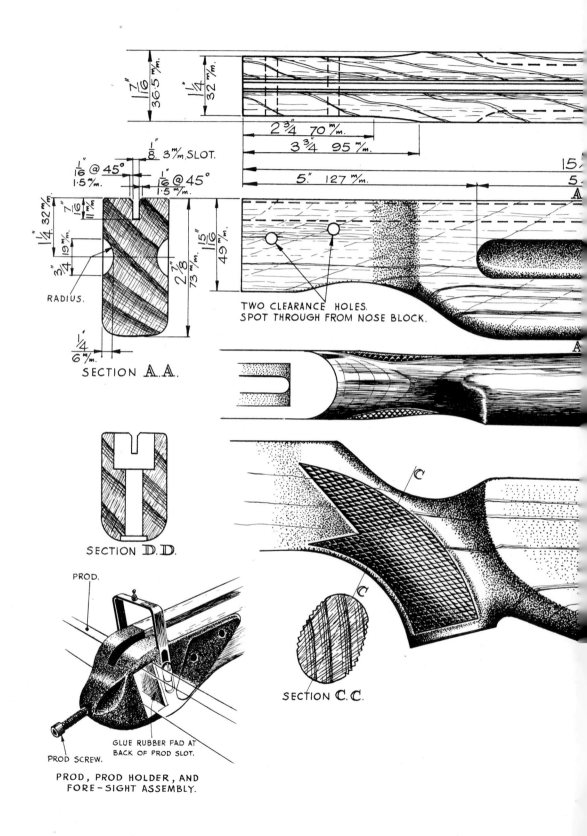

$\frac{7}{16}$" 36·5 $^m/_m$

$\frac{1}{4}$" 32 $^m/_m$

2$\frac{3}{4}$" 70 $^m/_m$

3$\frac{3}{4}$" 95 $^m/_m$

5." 127 $^m/_m$

$\frac{1}{8}$" 3 $^m/_m$ SLOT.

$\frac{1}{16}$" @ 45° 1·5 $^m/_m$

$\frac{1}{16}$" @ 45° 1·5 $^m/_m$

$\frac{1}{4}$" 32 $^m/_m$

$\frac{7}{16}$" 3 $^m/_m$

$\frac{3}{4}$" 19 $^m/_m$

$\frac{1}{4}$" 19 $^m/_m$

RADIUS.

2$\frac{1}{8}$" 73 $^m/_m$

$\frac{15}{16}$" 49 $^m/_m$

$\frac{1}{4}$" 6 $^m/_m$

SECTION A.A.

TWO CLEARANCE HOLES.
SPOT THROUGH FROM NOSE BLOCK.

SECTION D.D.

SECTION C.C.

C

PROD.

GLUE RUBBER PAD AT
BACK OF PROD SLOT.

PROD SCREW.

PROD, PROD HOLDER, AND
FORE-SIGHT ASSEMBLY.

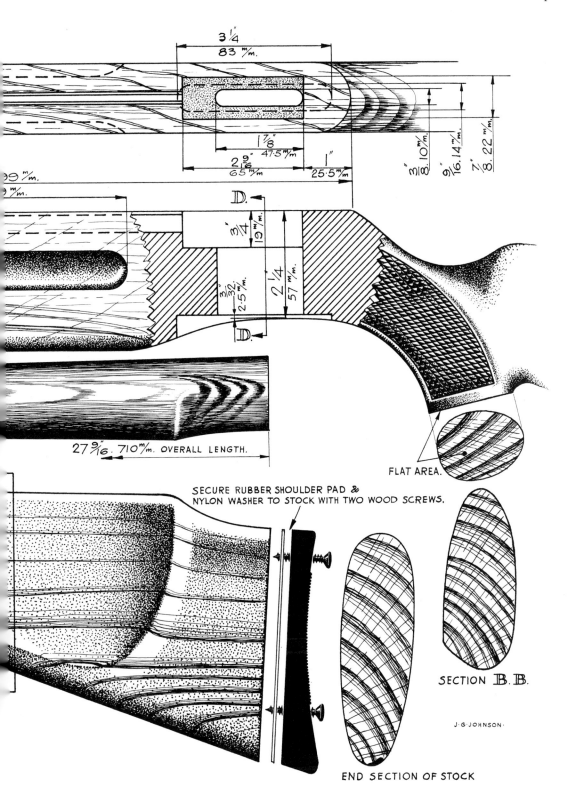

3 1/4
83 m/m.

1 7/8
47.5 m/m

2 9/16
65 m/m

1"
25.5 m/m.

3 m/10 m.
8

9 m/14 m.
16

7 m/8. 22 m/m.

D.

3"
19 m/m.
4

3"
32
2.5 m/m

2 1/4
57 m/m.

D.

27 9/16. 710 m/m. OVERALL LENGTH.

FLAT AREA.

SECURE RUBBER SHOULDER PAD &
NYLON WASHER TO STOCK WITH TWO WOOD SCREWS.

SECTION B.B.

J·G·JOHNSON·

END SECTION OF STOCK

59

5   The angle for fixing the bow or prod to the stock is critical. If the prod holder illustrated is not used, the basic problem to be overcome is as follows: The prod must be fixed below the top of the stock. When the bow or prod is drawn, the string should come to the centre of the bolt – much higher or lower will lift the bolt out of the slot as it drives forwards. As the bow is fired the string must slide forwards, but without rubbing too hard on the stock and causing friction.

Suitability of timbers   Timber used in a crossbow must be strong, resistant to splitting and wear, yet be reasonably light. The wood must also be very stable. Any timber used should be quarter sawn and have perfectly straight grain. Even a small knot may eventually cause the stock to warp, particularly if it is just on the edge of the stock.

Woods frequently used are walnut and mahogany. Increased stability is gained by laminating, a process which can be highly decorative if contrasting timbers are used. Decorative woods to be avoided when laminating are those with an oily nature, such as teak and rosewood.

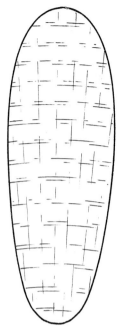

82   End section of stock

83   Oak and laurel. Lime 254mm × 380mm × 60mm (10in. × 15in. × 2⅜in.) Beeswax

84   Preliminary study for oak and laurel

Carving   Before actual carving can take place, it is necessary to plane the block into a perfectly rectangular prism. All parts which must be perfectly accurate are first made by normal cabinet making methods. The hole to take the trigger mechanism, the slot for the bolt and then both ends of the stock must be marked out from perfectly accurate surfaces. Only after this is it possible to let the artistic side of your personality run riot – but without breaking any of the basic principles of design or creating something which is uncomfortable to use.

A traditional example – Oak and Laurel leaves (83)

The design for this carving is based on oak and laurel leaves. These were selected for their symbolic interest and the suitability of the shapes for carving. Foliage to be avoided is that which does not have a simple and compact shape. Before starting work on the design, it is helpful to do some preliminary sketches of leaves (84).

Most technical problems are concerned with the fact that wood is prone to splitting along the grain. (Strength with the grain is twenty times greater than that across.) Owing to this, the strength advantage of a very low relief still firmly attached to the background is considerable. Even if the work is to take the form of a very low relief, the design should flow in the direction of the grain wherever possible.

In the design which I have used, the wood is lime and the grain runs left to right. Nearly all carvers allow the leaves to overlap and touch, so that the 'branches' do not hold the leaves together, it is the leaves which hold the branches. Nevertheless, the branches,

like several other parts with short grain, will snap easily if the utmost care is not taken. Although the working drawing shows these parts as being very delicate, they should be drawn onto the carving block as rather heavy. After the carving is almost complete, they can be carefully thinned down.

Framing
When making a low relief, it is worth considering the carving of an integral frame. This method of working makes the finished carving nearly as strong as the original piece of wood (85, 86 and 87).

85 *Amanda* Cherry
200mm × 137mm × 18mm
($7\frac{7}{8}$in. × $5\frac{3}{8}$in. × $\frac{3}{4}$in.)
Sealer and beeswax

86 Drawing an ellipse

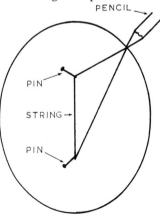

87 Early eighteenth century
medallion. Pine
The Victoria and Albert
Museum, London

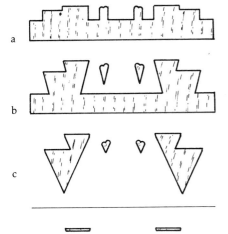

88 Stylized cross section of oak and
laurel leaves. Progression of quality

a

b

c

d

Suitability of timbers

1 *Lime.* This has a close grained and even consistency with a soft white colouring. It is the finest wood for this style of carving and a relief of 65mm (2½in.) is not too difficult to achieve.

2 *Sycamore.* Harder than lime but with a similar grain, it does not carve so delicately. Sycamore is almost too white for this subject and should be used in lower relief than lime.

3 *Walnut.* Similar carving properties to Sycamore but with a brown colouring.

4 *Oak.* Often used for this style of carving, but only in low relief. Oak has a coarse grain which tends to crumble around fine detail and prevents the wood polishing well. To compensate for the lack of sheen it is necessary to exaggerate the design.

5 *Pine.* Commonly available but do not be tempted. It's easier to cut firewood with an axe than a gouge.

6 Any other timber as similar as possible to lime. All wood should be free of knots and shakes, especially if the carving is to be delicately formed from a thick piece of wood.

Thickness of wood

Thick timber generally means more skill and work, but better quality. However, flowing curves and a good finish are preferable to an ambitious pile of splinters (88a). Thin soft wood is used by the beginner and the professional bodger. At the crudest level the design is pressed in. (Please don't bother to sue me, I have nothing!) (b). Greater skill and better quality carving timber allow the thickness to be increased, the design improved and undercutting started. This is the quality achieved by the average carver. (c) A high standard of achievement as the supporting background has now been dispensed with. (d) This is the final goal which crafts-men strive for. The leaves are delicate and of a constant thickness. Overlapping leaves do not touch unless strength is required.

Carving

When cutting a block of wood roughly to shape, several basic tools may be used. The chisel, spokeshave and related cutting tools will split the wood if used to cut in the wrong direction. Owing to the tendency of wood to split (also ivory, alabaster and many other materials), there are cases where the basic shape is most easily obtained by sawing or drilling. This is normally when you wish to remove large amounts, cut across or against the grain. There are no rigid rules as to which tool is most suitable to achieve any particular form. The suitability of each tool depends on:

1   The sculptor.
2   The material.
3   The form to be created.

   Following is the method of carving which I would suggest – it is not rigid.

1   Plane the selected piece of wood so that both sides are flat and parallel.
2   Transfer the design onto the wood. Do not forget to make the grain flow with the design, or mark delicate parts as thicker than they will be when the design is finished.
3   A bandsaw can be used to cut the outer shape. It is often helpful to leave a scrap piece of wood attached to the main bulk of the carving, for holding purposes. When a bandsaw is not available the best method is to use a hand drill fitted to a stand. Timber may be cut right through or to a predetermined depth. When working on a large scale the whole stand can be placed on the timber rather than *vice versa*. Internal parts and low relief carvings should be cut with the drill. See Chapter 3 for greater detail.
4   Clean off small portions of waste with a bevel edge chisel or inside ground gouge.
5   The highest parts are left, but everything else is next lowered relative to the design and thickness of the wood. At this stage the leaves are still flat, but without any detail on the surface. If applicable, the frame is now cut roughly to shape.

6   Each leaf is now carved in detail, but ignoring undercuts. Gouges are used for hollows, a bevel edge chisel for convex surfaces and a V tool for leaf veins and very sharp corners. The exact style of carving must be appropriate to the leaves or flowers used, the timber, tools available, taste and skills of the carver and of course the finances of the client. If the wood is lacking in quality, and fails to take a good polish, then vitality can be created by making highlights higher, hollows deeper and edges crisper. The whole form should now undulate with clean flowing lines. Those working in low relief should also carve the detail of the frame, if applicable.

7   Whether working with a truly three dimensional sculpture or a low relief carving, it is now necessary to finish the work to the point where it is almost ready for polishing. Coarse glasspaper should not be used; it merely removes any detail which you have put on. Good quality carving of this style should be finished with the cutting tools. However, I did finish the highlights of this carving by rubbing lightly, in the direction of the grain, with grade 240 garnet paper.

8   Undercutting is now started if possible. If a background is to be left, the undercutting must be carved out from the front using a bevel edge chisel and an inside ground gouge. Where the carving is to be completely three dimensional it should now be turned over.

To prevent damage to the already completed front, place the work in a shallow box lined with plastic foam. Use wedges under the foam wherever necessary to make the work stable. Cut gently with a small inside ground gouge. Five minutes extra carving is better than fifty hours making a replacement. Always cut with the grain and shape the wood as in illustration 88c. When the carving is mounted on a board, it will have to be screwed on with brass screws, so leave at least two parts which are thick enough for a screw to go into.

9   If you have the skill and confidence, continue to improve the delicacy with a small outside ground gouge. The difficulty now is that the work is too delicate to be clamped. Instead, it must be held on the foam with one hand and carved with the other, while trying to keep all parts of the body behind the cutting edge. If you intend cutting the leaves to the points where they are little thicker than real leaves, then the portions between the overlapping parts should be left solid until last. This is because it is the leaves which have the main structural strength.

10   Separation of the leaves is probably most easily carried out with a slim, long bladed penknife. This is only done to show your technical virtuosity to another expert, and to reduce the strength of the carving to almost nil.

In addition to carving in low relief and three dimensions, designs may also be incised, leaving the pattern surrounded by solid wood. A variation of this is intaglio, so that a cast of this

89 Butter pat *c* 1900. Sycamore
70mm × 90mm (2¾in. × 3½in.)
diameter
By courtesy of the Bell-Knight
Collection

90 Butter mould, ejector type
c 1900. Sycamore
133mm × 115mm (5¼in. × 4½in.)
diameter
By courtesy of the Bell-Knight
Collection

would form a relief pattern. Intaglio carving was common in the nineteenth century, so that 'carving' applied to furniture may consist of either glue and plaster or glue and sawdust.

Intaglio carved moulds were also commonly used for shaping butter. Flat pieces of wood form the butter into the basic shape, the wetted butter pat creating the raised design on the top of the butter (89). A second method was to press the butter into a wetted box mould before pressing it out (90).

Other examples of floral carving are the *Narcissus* (91), and the chair (93). The ash chair is particularly interesting, both in terms of design and technique. Most of the chair was made with a lathe, including the back legs up to the point where the ash twigs appear to grow out of the solid wood. Vibration was prevented during turning by attaching a counterbalance. After turning, the back legs were carved – the apparently turned parts at the tops of the legs was scraped smooth, the rest being left with the texture of the tool marks.

Further examples of floral carving are shown in illustrations 32, 58, 119 and 140.

91 Narcissus. Lime
230mm × 50mm × 50mm
(9in. × 2in. × 2in.)
Beeswax

92 Working drawing for Narcissus

93 Chair. Ash. Turned with
counterbalance and then carved
760mm (30in.)
Joe Dawes

St Stephen Stoned (94)

Although this is over 305mm (12in.) thick, it is in technique a low
relief carving. It is noteworthy that Grinling Gibbons kept this
carving himself for some time as part of his own collection, but
that the technique of making it was soon abandoned. Normally,
he laminated two or three boards one on top of the other. Smaller
parts of the carving such as flower heads and bird's wings were
then added, after completing larger sections of the work.

In this work, there are seventy biblical figures set against an
essay in architectural perspective – classical buildings, Corinthian
columns and arches. The wooden blocks, of which this carving is
composed, are glued side by side so that the springing apart is
readily seen. The actual buildings are of particular interest for they
appear fully three dimensional. In fact they have very little depth.
Exaggerated rather, they are almost like drawings on a flat sheet
of paper. This results in a most impressive effect when viewed
from the front with side lighting, and an interesting one when
viewed from the side.

The degree of relief varies even within this carving – the figures
in the foreground are three dimensional. As you go towards the
back of the scene, the relief is rapidly lowered until the sky in the
background is almost flat. *St Stephen Stoned* is a work of exceptionally
fine quality, both in technique and in the method of achieving a
three dimensional effect by the only practical means.

OPPOSITE
94 *St Stephen stoned* Grinling
Gibbons. Lime and lancewood
1m 830mm × 1m 335mm × 305mm
(6ft × 4ft 4½in. × 1ft)
The Victoria and Albert Museum,
London

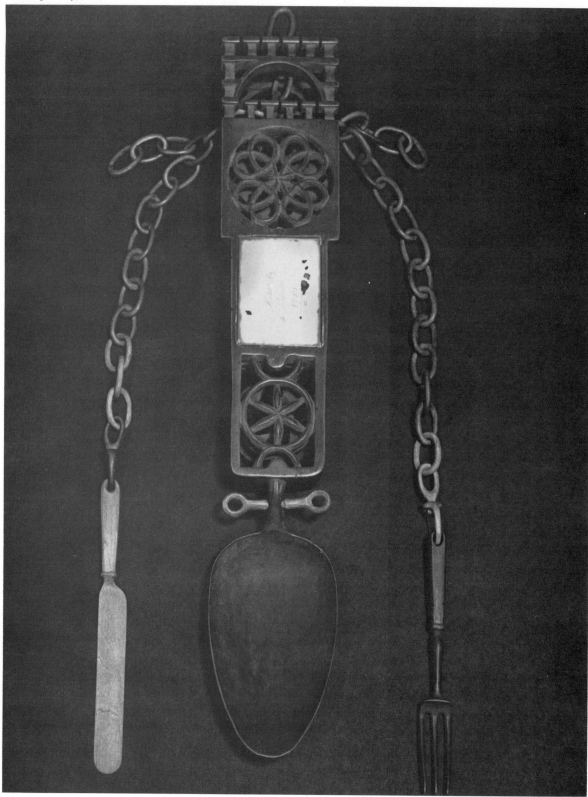

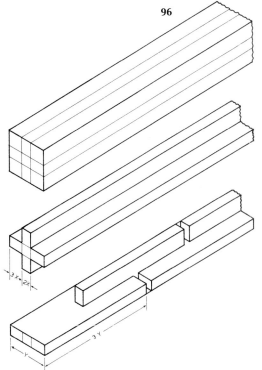

96

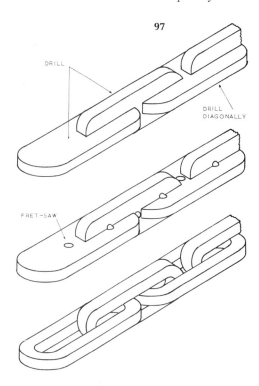

97

DRILL

DRILL DIAGONALLY

FRET-SAW

95 Welsh love spoon 1755. Sycamore 350mm (13¾in.)
Photographed after missing carving has been replaced, but before colouring and polishing

Welsh Love Spoon (95)
In this example the chains with knife and fork attached, were made separately. They were then attached to the main spoon with a wooden staple.

Carving a chain The method of carving a chain is variable – the proportions for the chain links in these diagrams are rather long and thin, but this makes carving easier.
1   A long square prism is first made and marked out as shown (96a).
2   With very small work a cutting gauge can be used to remove the waste wood. Larger work requires a rebate plane (96b).
3   After marking out with dividers, a dovetail saw is used to form the basic shape of the links. The gap between any two links in the same plane is the diameter of the smallest drill through which a fret saw blade will pass or an arbitary measurement to allow the use of a knife (96c).
4   Drill straight through between the links or use a thin bladed knife to separate adjoining links in the same plane. Drilling diagonally is the first step to separating any two links in different planes (97a).
5   A fret saw is the most efficient method of creating the basic shape inside the links. However, a penknife with a very long slim blade is the only tool which I find satisfactory for finally separating the links (97b).
6   Use a knife to radius internal corners, then external corners (97c).

Inside the spoon, under the piece of glass on which it says 'Made by a Prisoner 1755' (it must have been a long sentence), are rows of beads, completely enclosed within the carving. The basic principle of carving these is similar to that of making the chain – fine drills and a slim, long bladed knife being used.

Joints into the knife and fork, and the swivel joints just above these are probably best carried out with only a knife.

Carved fireplace (98)

The actual surround was first made by almost normal cabinet making methods. Mouldings were cut with a scratch stock and the surround assembled before applying the carving. This was fixed on from the back with brass screws.

Sudden or prolonged heat is the most serious practical consideration, possibly applied at the end of a long winter holiday. Owing to this, quarter sawn boards should be used wherever possible. Wide boards need to be jointed with the direction of the annual rings alternating (99). It is also wise to use strengthening battens, but these must only be rigidly fixed at one point. Button head screws can then pass through slots into the surround, so allowing movement between the parts (100).

98 Carved fireplace. Lime. When this fireplace was installed, a marble surround was fitted inside the wooden frame. This is indicated by the light line on the working drawing 1m 42mm × 1m 220mm × 190 mm (41in. × 48in. × 7½in.) Polyurethane and wax

WIDE BOARDS

WARP

Movement between the wide horizontal board and the two uprights is allowed by the method of jointing. Mortise and tenons near the middle are rigidly glued with heat resistant adhesive, the extremities of the wide board sliding in grooves. The moulding under the shelf is glued to the shelf and the uprights of the surround, but not to the horizontal board. The shelf is screwed to the rest of the surround.

NARROW BOARDS JOINTED

99   WARP LESS

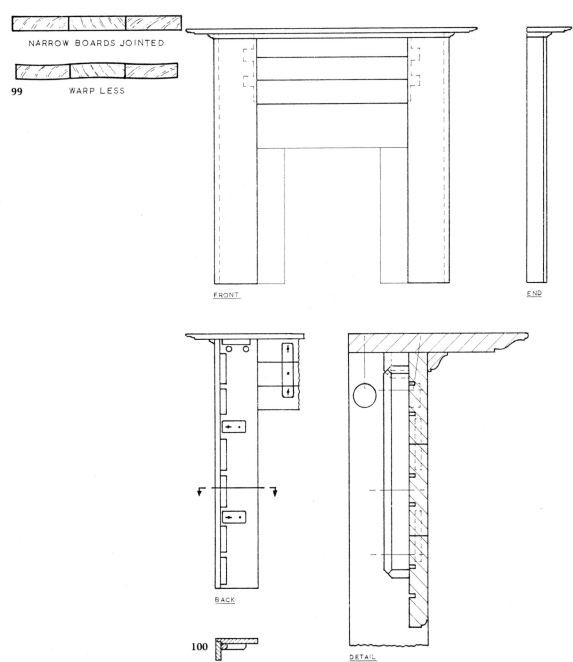

FRONT

END

BACK

100

DETAIL

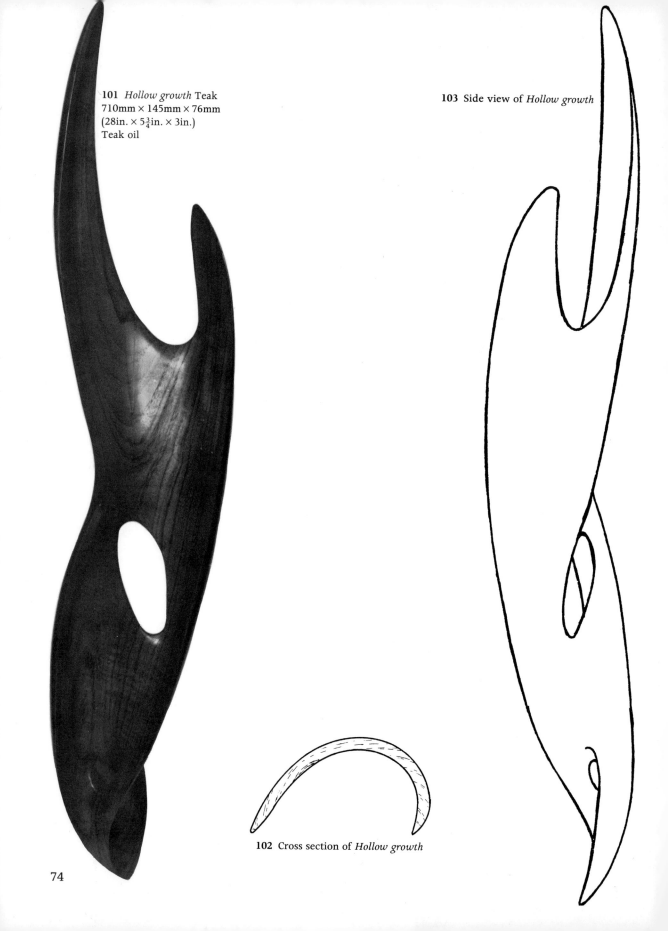

101 *Hollow growth* Teak
710mm × 145mm × 76mm
(28in. × 5¾in. × 3in.)
Teak oil

103 Side view of *Hollow growth*

102 Cross section of *Hollow growth*

A shell form – Hollow Growth (101)

This is a non-representational form inspired by a small scrap of wood found on the workshop floor. This was re-shaped and then used as a study for the full scale sculpture. Slight modifications were made in the larger work to allow for differences in grain structure. (That's my excuse and I'm sticking to it.)

The concept is of a delicate and subtly twisting form, suitable for the interior of a reasonably large and elegant house. Sculpture to be sited outside should be larger, stronger and more solid. Although the delicate shell form is too difficult for the unskilled wood sculptor, the concept can be used in a more solid design.

Non-representational sculpture is still governed by formal laws. In *Hollow Growth*, the longer arm must be of sufficient length to balance the bulge below it. The shorter arm reduces the long gentle curve to a size where the visual impact balances the complexity of the other side. In the middle, the asymetrical hole pierces the form, emphasising depth and breaking up the large central mass. Note also that the shape of the hole harmonizes with the overall form. The lower hole is used to link the larger mass to the small lower protrusion. This also emphasizes the slight spiralling motion started in the larger arm. The overall effect hints at something more than a relief shape, hopefully making the onlooker want to turn the sculpture around and view it from different positions (103). When there are a greater number of different positions to study the sculpture from, the greater will be the interest. For this reason, sculpture is normally best when it is asymetrical, for a symetrical mass is only using half the available viewpoints.

Hollow Growth may either lie down on a plinth, or be suspended on a fine nylon thread. Suspension allows the work to be gently rotated by the air currents within a room.

A shell form – December (104)

Design   The design illustrated is one of a series which I have carved, inspired by the shell of an egg. This type of form excites my childish curiosity for looking inside things and handling smooth rounded objects. Combined with this is the inherent strength of the shape, and its potential delicacy. When designing sculptures of this type, the most effective are often the simplest. It is the deceptive simplicity which creates the problems, as the slightest superfluous curve or mark destroys the whole concept. Crisp edges are another headache, as these demand a hard, straight grained timber; lime is too soft.

Owing to the delicate nature of the shell style of work it is necessary to carefully consider how it will be mounted. In the example December there is a thick portion at the bottom from which a $1\frac{1}{2}$mm ($\frac{1}{16}$in.) diameter stainless steel pin joins it to the base. Alternatives are to lay the sculpture down, or suspend it from the ceiling on a fine nylon thread.

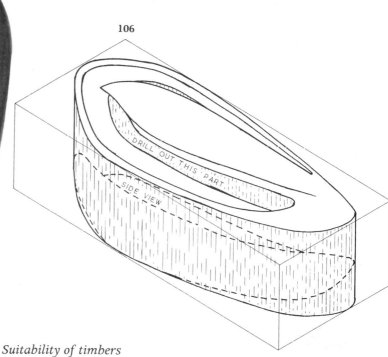

106

104 *December* Greenheart
290mm × 120mm × 75mm
(11½in. × 4¾in. × 3in.)
Button polish and beeswax

105 Cross section of *December*

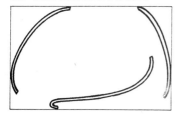

Suitability of timbers

1   *Sycamore*. Moderately hard, straight and close grained, it is a soft white in colour and carves very well.

2   *Cherry*. Capable of taking an excellent finish.

3   *Walnut*. Similar to sycamore but with a brown colouring. The more open grain removes the silky lustre of sycamore. Beware of shakes.

4   *Pear*. Fine grained and carves well. Very pale colour. Only available in small sizes.

5   *Yew*. This timber has many flaws, despite which the extremely variable grain and colouring are often well worth a little extra work.

6   Any other timber as similar as possible to sycamore.

Carving

1   Plane two surfaces of the wood flat and parallel.

2   Copy the design onto the wood, ensuring that the grain flows with the design.

3   Cut around the drawing, preferably with a bandsaw or pillar drill, ensuring that the edges are clean and square (106).

4   Where the design is to be pierced right through, a drill should be used. It is faster, easier and more accurate than a bow saw. The most efficient drill types for this job are the saw tooth machine centre bit or a lip and spur drill.

5   The side view of the sculpture must now be drawn onto one of the newly cut surfaces (106, dotted line).

6   All flat surfaces are now cut away and smoothed off, probably with the chisel and flat spokeshave. At this stage the sculpture is still simple and angular.

7   Hollows, other than where it is pierced right through, are shallowly cut in.

8   The external shape is now carved in detail. With small scale work, garnet paper grade 120 or finer, with a glasspaper block can be used to rub the sculpture to highlight blemishes. Most of the external finishing is completed with a bevel edge chisel, a very finely set spokeshave and a sharp gouge. Finally smooth of with grade 240 garnet paper. Even minute flaws will glare when the sculpture is polished. When working on a large scale, the circular plane (020C) (107), will save many hours of work and give a smooth flowing line.

9   Hollowing is now started. It can normally be carried out with a gouge, thinning the wood to whichever degree suits the design and the sculptor. Parts which should not be excessively thinned are end grain (which is very weak) and any part where the sculpture will be jointed to the base.

107 Circular plane

From the aesthetic viewpoint, the walls should be thin and of an even thickness (108d). However, few sculptors have the skill to achieve this and even fewer clients have the ability to appreciate the extra cost. Owing to this, the centre of the shell is normally left quite thick and only the edges are thinned, so reducing the time and skill involved (108c).

10   Smoothing the inside requires considerable patience and an extremely sharp set of tools. Radius the corners of your gouges (19), Chapter 3, Modifying Tools, and use the flattest possible, carefully removing high spots. Continue until the internal hollow follows the external surface; a curved gouge will be particularly useful here. Smooth with grade 240 garnet paper. With some of the extremely hard and close grained woods, a much finer abrasive is needed – I sometimes use grade 600.

11   All mad nuts who really want their shell form to be as thin as, or thinner than a real egg shell, should continue as follows:

Slowly continue hollowing the inside until a bright spotlight, placed a few inches from the wood, shows dimly through. Thin any part of the sculpture which shows as a shadow. Yes, it's true, I am mad. By this stage the wood is beginning to get a bit thin and something must be placed behind the work. This should be directly opposite the cutting edge of the gouge to prevent any stress. I use my fingers but, as I shouldn't tell you to take such dangerous steps, try to find something else.

Next, soak the sculpture in a non-drying oil – cooking oil is excellent. Cover a small light with black card through which there is a small hole. Sit in a blacked out room, the light between your feet, the sculpture between your eyes and the light. Working like this the wood becomes translucent and it is easy to see exactly how the work is progressing. Continue to thin the sculpture as long as your confidence or the wood lasts.

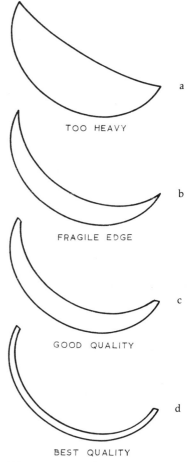

a

TOO HEAVY

b

FRAGILE EDGE

c

GOOD QUALITY

d

BEST QUALITY

108 Progression of quality

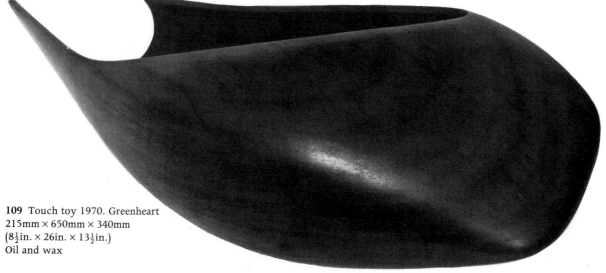

109 Touch toy 1970. Greenheart
215mm × 650mm × 340mm
(8½in. × 26in. × 13½in.)
Oil and wax

Touch Toy '70 (109), is also hollowed out like an egg shell, the tools and techniques being almost identical with that of *December*. Size caused the main difference in technique, the preliminary shaping of the large sculpture being mainly carried out with an adze. Finishing also needed a larger scale of tools, the largest and flattest gouges being used inside the form. Sculpture in this style may or may not be representational, the wings of birds often being made by these methods. Further examples of the use of shell forms can be seen in illustrations 13, 38, 50 and 91.

The human form – a mechanical toy (110a, b)

This example is a Japanese boxwood toy dating from the early twentieth century. It is made in several separate parts and assembled,

110a, b Japanese mechanical toy. Early twentieth century. Carved and turned box with ivory, bone and ebony 125mm × 160mm × 75mm (5in. × 6¼in. × 3in.)

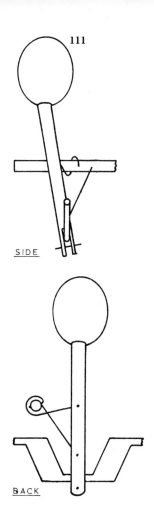

111

SIDE

BACK

some joints being glued and others pinned. Between the two large wheels is a crankshaft which is cut from solid timber (111). The long neck is linked directly to this, and is so raised and lowered as the wheels turn. A series of ridges carved horizontally on the neck below the chin produce a grating noise as the head moves. As the crankshaft moves forwards at its maximum height, it throws the head back. The ivory tongue, being loosely fitted into the head can then fall forwards, although it appears to be mechanically protruded. Thread holds the tongue in this position until the head starts to lower, and the features relax into less grotesque positions.

Movement of the arm to bang the gong is caused by a length of thread pinned into the neck just below its lowest visible point. The thread is then wrapped around and pinned into the arm, and from there passes to the base of the neck where it is again pinned in.

The precise method of holding a thread in place is to drill a small hole into the wood. Thread is then passed into this hole, and a small tapered wooden pin is pressed in to hold it tight.

A crisp angular style –
The Bowler (112)
Design This example is of a bowler, the ball having just left the right hand. The proportions of the figure have been altered; the head is slightly smaller, so that the shoulders appear stronger. Also, the legs have been lengthened, again to

112 *The Bowler*
Imbuia (Brazilian walnut)
248mm × 152mm × 70mm
($9\frac{3}{4}$in. × 6in. × $2\frac{3}{4}$in.)
Oil

make the figure appear more powerful. It is in this attempt to portray the strength and power that I have given this figure a crisp angular style.

The stance of this figure has been selected for two reasons; one is that there is no serious problem with short grain. The second and most important consideration is the aesthetic one. When the human figure is in this position it is possible for the eye to follow the lines of movement through the limbs. It is this optical movement which helps to create vitality and interest.

The Bowler poses different problems from the others in this series. Possibly the most obvious difference is in the tools required; at no point were any sculptor's tools used, but instead the traditional cabinet makers equipment. The second difference is in the amount of skill required. Some of the previous sculptures discussed in this series could have been made, without the refinements, by a beginner. Owing to the very straight edges, *The Bowler* needs a fair degree of patience and precision to prevent it looking like the remnants of a mouse's dinner.

Another difference between this sculpture and many others is in the quantity and quality of preliminary drawing (113). With an 'abstract' it is easier, although not necessarily more justifiable, to allow changes between the original design and the finished sculpture to pass unnoticed. With a sculpture based on a human figure, there are far more people who feel able to make destructive criticism. Might I suggest that the complete beginner select a figure which has a less complex form.

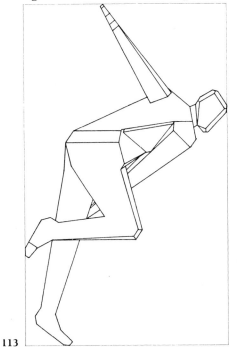
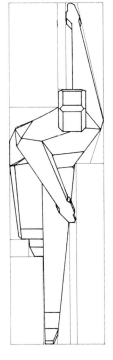

113

114 *Baby Boy Hepworth*
Bronze cast from
Greenheart pattern
610mm × 75mm ×
75mm (24in. × 3in. ×
3in.)

Suitability of timbers   This angular style of sculpture depends largely on precision for its impact, and this can only be achieved with quality tools and hard materials.

1   *Imbuia.* A hard timber which takes an excellent polish. The colour mellows to a rich brown with an oil polish or age.

2   *Pear.* A pale wood with a fine even texture.

3   *Cherry.* Light brown and very suitable, if you can find a piece without distinctive grain.

4   Almost any hard and close grained wood without bold figuring, which will destroy the lines of the sculpture.

Carving

1   Accurately plane both sides of the wood flat, parallel and to the thickness of the figure when seen head on.

2   Draw the side view onto the wood, obtaining the best compromise possible with the short grain running across limbs.

3   A bandsaw could be used to cut out the view when seen from the side. This particular example was shaped with a tenon saw and dovetail saw for the finer detail. Accuracy is best checked with an Ever True trysquare.

4   Pierce through the centre of the wood with a pillar drill. Omit this part if an efficient mechanical drill is not available.

5   Use tenon and dovetail saws to cut away the outline as seen from the front. The faintly drawn lines on the front view of illustration 113 show the main cuts made to create this elevation. All these cuts should be marked on with a ruler, trysquare, marking gauge and marking knife. The theory behind this deviation from standard practice is that it is easy to correct mistakes on paper, and then make a few decisive cuts. An alternative is to nibble away for an interminable age, creating a miniature masterpiece from a mammoth block of wood.

6   The main part still to remove is the undercutting where the right arm crosses the front of the body. This, like the other small parts still to remove, must be completed with a series of small chisel cuts. Check frequently with a steel ruler to ensure accuracy.

7   Where an abrasive paper is needed, it must be as fine as possible. Anything coarser than grade 240 will quickly round the corners. For a very fine finish with a very hard wood, it will be necessary to use at least grade 400. To prevent corners being rounded, it is best to wrap and glue the abrasive paper around a flat piece of wood.

Another example of a crisp angular style is *Baby Boy Hepworth* (114). This bronze was made by the sand casting process, working from a Greenheart pattern. Internal surfaces are polished and lacquered, the exterior has a dark patina.

Other examples of the human form

Human figures can be made in a wide variety of styles – possibly the simplest shown is the head by J. Karski (115). There is no refinement, but the almost primitive style has great character. Branches portray the hair in a most unusual way and the combination of polished and textured wood adds further interest.

Punch and Judy (116), are more refined but still simple. They have rag bodies, turned legs and crudely carved feet. Even the heads are simple – main features are the noses and chins which are boldly shaped. In comparison, the other features are shallowly carved, then painted to make them more realistic.

115 Head. Lilac
965mm (38in.)
J Karski

116 Late nineteenth century Punch and Judy puppets. Probably lime. Heads, hands and feet carved and painted, legs turned
407mm (16in.)
By courtesy of the Bell-Knight Collection

83

117 Dancers. Plane
305mm (12in.)
Donald Potter

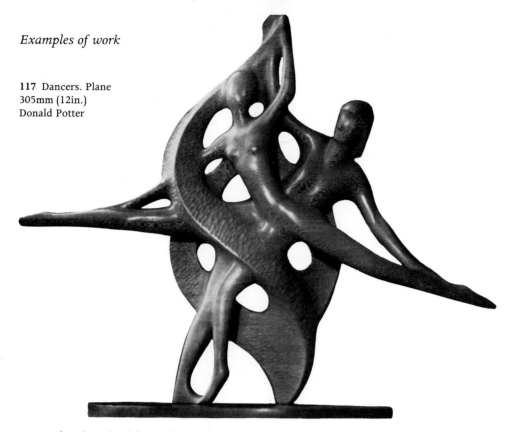

Simple, but highly refined, is the sculpture *Dancers* (117). With its streamlined and fluid movement there is little detail but great vitality. Even the tool marks on the flowing drapes are calculated – carefully placed and helping to lead the eye to the centre of the work.

In contrast with *Dancers, The Jesuit Saint* (118), is a preliminary sketch which gains much of its character from the roughness of the tool markings. There is no calculated refinement but instead an almost child-like, yet highly skilled, technique. Beside the Saint – either St Aloysius Gonzaga or St Francis Borgia – is the figure of a putto, who holds a skull. Although crudely formed this sketch nevertheless has the essence of a completed work, with the basic proportions and movement in the invisible line which flows through the centre.

Misericord seats in churches (121), may again show an almost child-like simplicity. *The Jesuit Saint* is carved from pear and so shows more lightness. Oak, from which these seats are almost invariably made, has a coarser grain. It is the open grain which necessitates a greater heaviness to prevent crumbling and bold forms to compensate for the wood's lack of ability to take a good finish. In consequence, this head although finished does make an interesting comparison with *The Jesuit Saint*.

In contrast to the immediately preceding photographs of the human form, the following are much more naturalistic.

The Charioteer (120), is a bronze cast, almost certainly made from a wooden pattern, possibly something similar to sycamore.

118 Jesuit saint. Pear
238mm (9⅜in.)
Victoria and Albert Museum, London

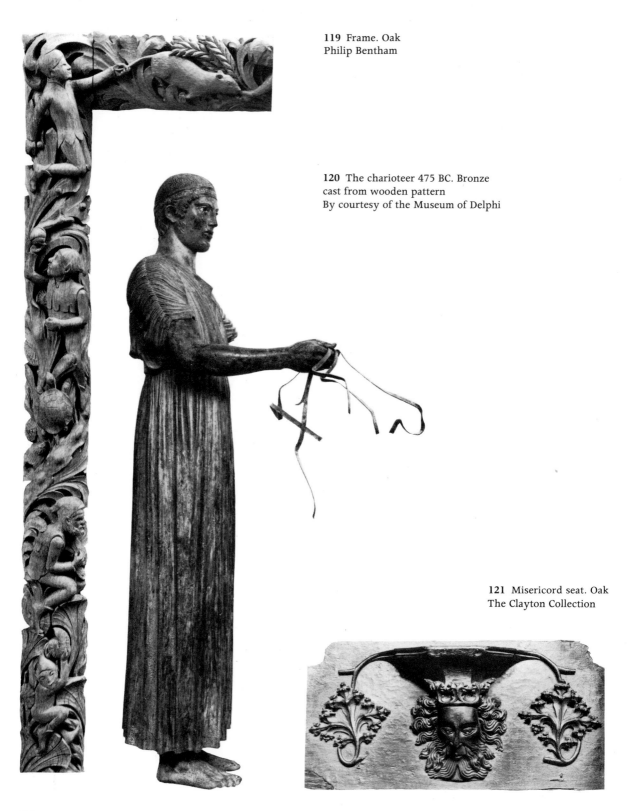

119 Frame. Oak
Philip Bentham

120 The charioteer 475 BC. Bronze
cast from wooden pattern
By courtesy of the Museum of Delphi

121 Misericord seat. Oak
The Clayton Collection

It is of a charioteer who, having won his race, is on the final lap of victory. The sculpture is as naturalistic as possible, even down to the inlayed eyes and the detail of the fingernails.

Death (122) can hardly be called lifelike, but it was certainly made by a seventeenth-century Bavarian with a knowledge of anatomy. The bow, arrows and quiver are not original as can be seen by the comparative crudeness of technique in the carving and the discrepency between the positions of the hands and the bow and arrows.

The three oak carvings (119, 123 and 124), are different but related. Although detailed there is, like the misericord, a boldness of form which is characteristic of work in oak. To a limited degree, many of the tool marks have been left. Subtle tool marks add life to a rather plain material and detract from the slight heaviness of form caused by the coarse grained timber.

122 *Death c* 1675. Lime 280mm (11in.) Victoria and Albert Museum, London

123 Willow dryad. Oak M Joyce Bidder

124 Saint Michael. Oak
660mm (26in.)
M Joyce Bidder

Box is a very hard, close and even-grained timber. Owing to this it is capable of taking extremely fine detail and a high polish. These facts are easily shown by the sculpture *Fear* (125). The strength of wood across the grain is on average, one twentieth of the strength with the grain. One result of this is that it would be impossible for an amateur to carve the fingers of the left hand. Even for a skilled craftsman there are few timbers which could take this form of cross grained detail. In terms of design, skill and technique the sculpture is excellent – completely regardless of whether or not you like the subject matter.

The Charioteer also exhibits considerable skills, but the pose is calm and relaxed. Much of the serenity is portrayed by the way the Charioteer's clothing hangs. With *Fear* the clothing does not fall gracefully, but is creased in a disorganized fashion. As opposed to *Dancers*, the limbs are also positioned to prevent any smoothly flowing optical line. It is the disorganized and cringing position of the limbs, combined with the lack of any directional movement, which portrays the emotion of fear as much as the facial expression.

Apart from the immediately preceding photographs, the human form is also portrayed in illustrations 4c, 37, 85, 87 and 94.

Animal carving – Polar Bears playing (126)

The timber used in this example is sycamore, the creamy white colour and fine texture being harmonious with the bear's fur. There is no basic style, just scaling, copying and sweat. Owing to the simplicity of the design, a detailed drawing of the side view is sufficient, and carbon paper may be used to copy this on to the wood.

Sawing or drilling can achieve the outer shape, the spaces between the bears by drilling.

To draw the side views on to the newly cut surfaces I sketched a centre line for each bear, one on each side of the block. On either side of these centre lines I drew the outline of each bear. This is the method I would recommend for a small simple form. On a larger scale or with a greater complexity I would suggest an accurate drawing of both front and side views.

Carving can be carried out with a selection of gouges and a wide chisel. The scale of this carving is very small and the problem was to omit confusing detail without destroying the essence of the animals. In this instance there is no detail other than the canine teeth. However, on a larger scale I would have introduced claws, eyes and the texture of fur.

Different sculptors use different methods of depicting fur, some of which are shown:

127 (a) A V tool makes fine lines but these are very crisp. Distinctive and often suitable for an animal with bristly fur.

127 (b) A fine gouge or veiner gives a similar but softer effect – much more suitable for an animal of this type.

125 *Fear* Early eighteenth century
Austrian. Box
246mm (9⅝ in.)
Victoria and Albert Museum, London

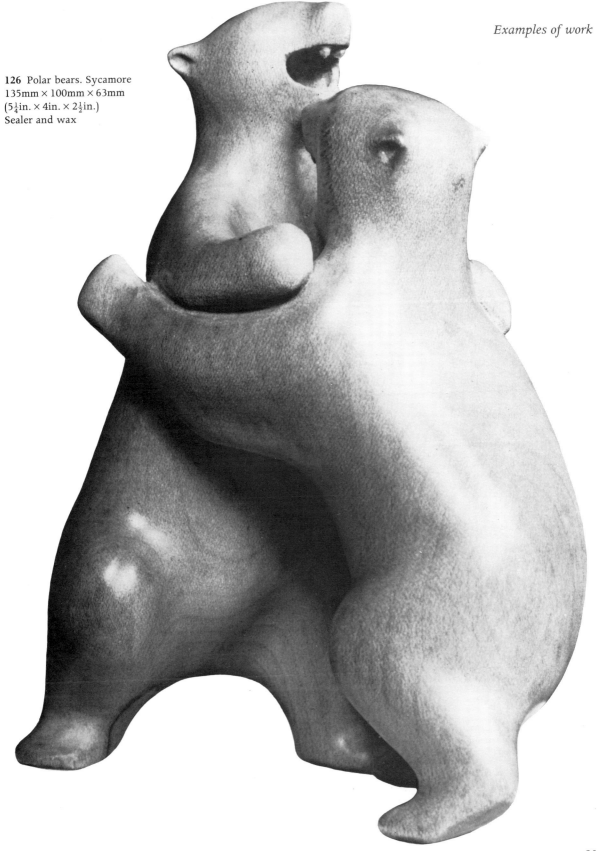

126 Polar bears. Sycamore
135mm × 100mm × 63mm
(5¼in. × 4in. × 2½in.)
Sealer and wax

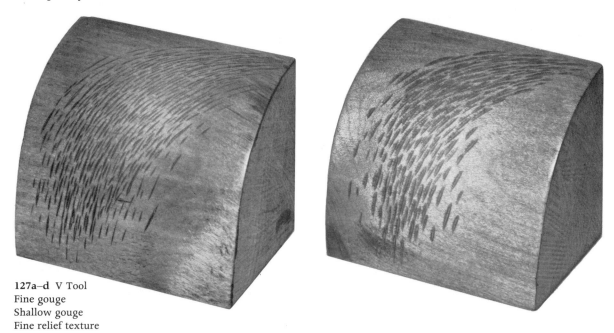

127a–d V Tool
Fine gouge
Shallow gouge
Fine relief texture

128 Young bear.
Burmese teak
205mm × 325mm × 153mm
(8in. × 12¾in. × 6in.)
A Mandl

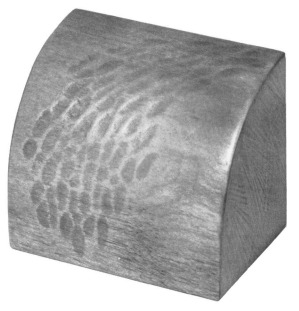

127 (c)   Shallow gouges give a much more subtle effect but, for this example, is as unsuitable as the harsh lines of the V tool. It is, however, ideal for depicting the finer feathers on birds.

127 (d)   When studied, fur is not a flat surface with a series of grooves in it. Instead, it is a slightly undulating surface with a series of smooth and subtle undulations above it. Despite the labour involved, this would be my favourite texture if I carried out this sculpture on a larger scale.

Similar to the *Polar Bears Playing* is *The Young Bear* (128), which portrays the bulk and weight of this lumbering creature. Although on a much larger scale, this sculpture still does not have any detail on it, as this would cause a clash with the bold figuring.

A most interesting work is *The Otter* (129). It is carried out on a much larger scale than *The Young Bear* and so, although the figuring is bold, the surface is textured.

129 Otter. Pitch pine
150mm × 1m 67mm
(6in. × 3ft 6in.)
Richard Fisher

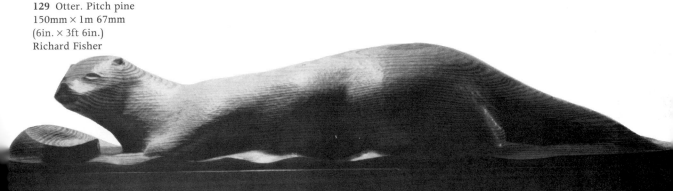

Few woodcarvings are functional, but a pleasant exception is the top from the Late Victorian walking stick (130). The stick part was a branch and the handle was shaped from the fork at the bottom – the carver formed this into the head of a Bulldog and then inlayed this with glass eyes.

Rocking Horse (131), is an imaginative concept. The photograph is self-explanatory and is included mainly because the sculpture is so unusual. Compare the method of texturing the tail with the tool marks on the other animals.

Animal forms have also been depicted in illustrations 42, 48, 119 and 142.

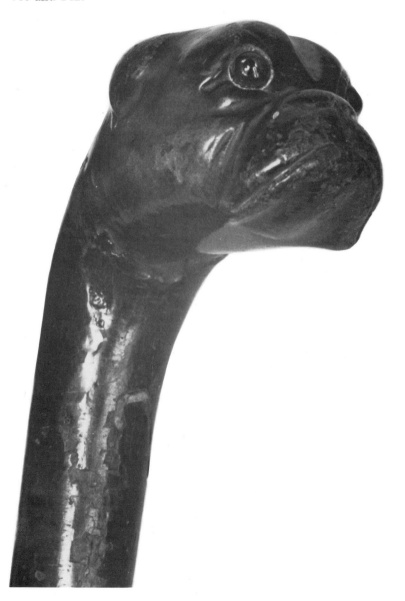

130 Late nineteenth century bull dog head of walking stick. Carved branch with glass eyes
By courtesy of the Bell-Knight Collection

131 Rocking horse. Cherry
505mm (1ft 8in.)
Donald Potter

Birds

Birds are a popular subject with woodcarvers yet this generally means a static pose with folded wings (132 and 133), or a rather heavy bird with as much ability to fly as a lump of lead. Alternatively, the wings may be jointed onto the body of the bird – which always creates a harsh line where the grain changes direction.

132 Owl. Rosewood
273mm × 172mm × 127mm
(10¾in. × 6¾in. × 5in.)
Beeswax
A Mandl

133 Woodpecker. Walnut
230mm (9in.)
George Taylor

134a, b Owl. Yew
660mm × 455mm × 305mm
(26in. × 18in. × 12in.)
Silicone wax
Ferelyth Wills

There are few satisfactory ways around this problem except to select your style and create the best that your skills and material will allow. Using the fork of a tree is one solution, but this timber is very difficult to work (134a and b). Another way of reducing the problem of short grain is to have the bird among trees, rushes or, as in the example of *Swan Lake*, the bird is standing on its own reflection (13).

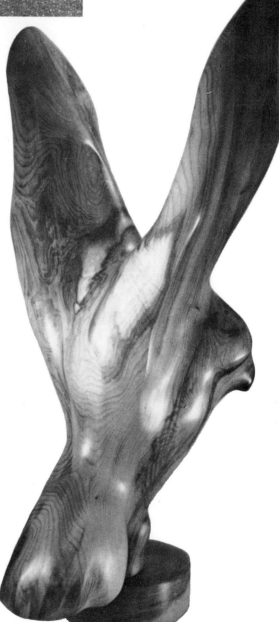

135 *Feeding Tern* Teak on stainless steel base
290mm × 160mm × 65mm
(11½in. × 6¼in. × 2½in.)
Teak oil

Some birds do, however, sometimes go into a position where there is no serious problem with short grain. The sculpture *Feeding Tern* is based on several species of tern. From each species, the basic characteristics which were most suitable for carving were taken.

The tern feeds by flying slowly above the surface of the water. When food is spotted the tail is lowered to act as a brake, the wings are raised and the bird falls. When the bird touches the water it picks up the food. There is immediately a vigorous downward wingbeat which lifts the bird up to continue normal flight. In this rather simplified form the downward wingbeat has just started (135 and 136).

99

136

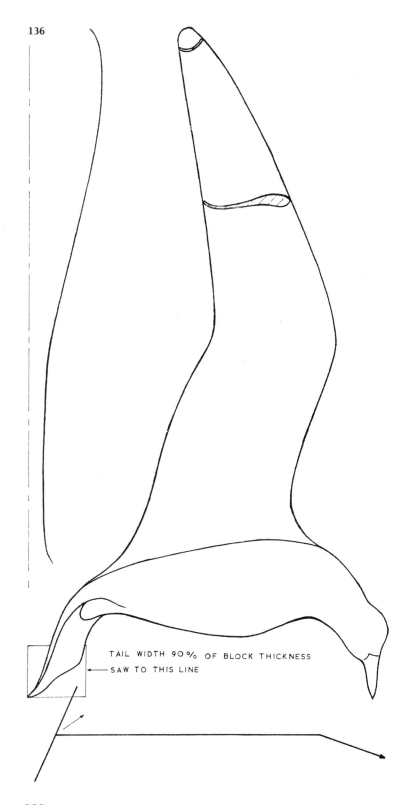

TAIL WIDTH 90% OF BLOCK THICKNESS

← SAW TO THIS LINE

6 Finishing

137 (a) Section through wood after sanding

(b) After wetting

When magnified, wood has a structure similar to that of a bundle of straws. After using a very fine abrasive paper or steel wool, some of the wood is compressed into the open tubes of the grain. Moisture in the air and timber will later make this compressed wood swell and spoil the smooth finish of the sculpture (137). To prevent this happening I recommend that the sculpture is now thoroughly washed. When dry the swollen wood can be cut off with abrasive paper grade 320, or steel wool grade 0000. Some of the hard and very close grained timbers will need even finer abrasives such as grade 500.

Flat areas are best smoothed off with an abrasive paper, but textures and fine detail will be rubbed off unless steel wool is used. An exception is oak where paper should always be used – fragments of steel wool will break off and be left in the grain. Steel will react with the tannic acid in oak and produce dark stains, It is for the same reason that any steel screws should now be removed and replaced by brass ones.

A glazed finish is unsuitable for wood sculpture as it destroys the grain and dominates the shape. Instead, a subtle sheen tends to emphasize the form by creating gentle highlights. However, the degree of polish is variable, simple forms tend to need a higher finish to create interest where detail is lacking. Unless an oil polish is to be used, a sealing agent is usually necessary to prevent dirt from entering the grain before waxing.

While the sealing is being carried out, two precautions must be taken:

1   Dust in the atmosphere can be trapped in the polish. It is preferable if a separate room can be used for polishing. Failing this, do not carry out any glasspapering immediately before or after polishing – unless you want a textured finish.

2   Moisture trapped under the polish will whiten it, occasionally to the point where the wood looks as though it has been sprayed with white paint. Prevention of this is simply by keeping the work and the polish in a warm dry room for some time. Polishing is then carried out in the same room, and the high temperature maintained until the polish is dry.

The full polishing process is given in confusing detail in most woodwork text books. Basically, the polish is wiped on with a rubber – a piece of fine cotton inside which is a pad of cotton wool containing some polish. This gives a thin and even film as the rubber is used with a circular motion to pack the pores of the timber, and then wiped off along the grain.

A rubber is satisfactory for smooth areas without fine detail, but for complex areas with deep undercutting, the alternatives are a mop or an airbrush. A mop is rather like an artist's brush with very fine and soft hairs, but on a rather larger scale. Despite the softness of the hair, the polish must be well diluted and sparingly applied to prevent a thick glazed film.

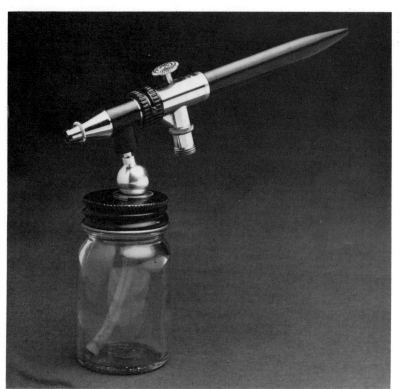

Airbrushes are simply a small but versatile form of spray gun, giving superior results on small or complex work. They can be used to apply stain, polish or wax, and are particularly useful for restoration – disguising colour variations between original and replacement timber. Of the many airbrushes on the market, *The Sprite* has proved to be one of the most efficient (138). When finishing work, such as puppets, it is possible to draw fine lines of detail or subtle shading and highlights. The source of power may be a compressor or can of aerosol propellant, so that any fluid is blown into the fine detail and even into the pores of the wood. In contrast, thick polishes carelessly brushed on will only form a thick skin over the wood.

Button polish is an effective sealing agent on brown timber. For a wood which is extremely dark or light, a bleached shellac or cellulose is more effective. The secret of obtaining a quality finish is to work in a warm room, apply the sealing agent as thinly as possible, allow it to dry and then rub it off with fine abrasive paper or steel wool. Continue repeating this process until the hollow fibres, of which the grain is composed, are packed with polish. When the wood begins to shine it is ready for the final polish. This is diluted at least to half strength. When thoroughly hard, the final coat is rubbed down with grade 0000 steel wool, saturated in wax polish to reduce the abrasiveness. Rub with a clean soft cloth to complete the polishing.

If the waterproof properties of polyurethane are required, the high gloss type is recommended owing to its superior properties. The glaze must of course be removed with a fine abrasive. Despite instructions on the tin about brushing, I would recommend that the polyurethane be applied very thinly. This is achieved by working with warm materials in a warm room and using a very firm rubber, or spraying if you are able to obtain the correct grade of polish.

Waxing

After sealing, a wax is necessary for indoor work. Beeswax polish can be made by grating a block of pure beeswax (obtainable from some chemists or a beekeeper) into an airtight jar. Add turpentine to this and leave in a warm place until the wax dissolves – **caution:** it is **highly inflammable.** The consistency should be that of a thick paste, rather like butter on a hot day. Owing to its efficiency as a grain filler, beeswax can give a high finish, even on open grained timber which has not been fully sealed.

Wax produces a soft and subtle sheen which is suitable for use on antiques and the harder, more highly figured timbers. Also useful for complex work where there is ample interest in the shaping of the wood. Silicone wax is a hard wearing wax which gives a high polish. The silicone gives a slightly harder appearance than that of pure wax, making it unsuitable for some traditional work. It is however satisfactory for use in more modern homes, particularly where a rather plain timber is used to create a sculpture of a simple form.

I am strongly prejudiced against aerosols. One reason is because this expensive type of polish will react unfavourably with traditional waxes and may mean that re-finishing is necessary. Also, some of these modern polishes are quite useless for our purpose.

Oil finishes

Oil finishes are simple to apply and are most suitable for complex work, as there is no rubbing down between coats. The basic procedure is to rub the oil well in, and remove the surplus with a clean cloth. Ordinary cooking oil (corn oil) is best for salad and fruit dishes, as it does not affect the taste of the food. Repeat the oiling whenever the wood begins to look dry. Do not wash the carving with hot water, or use detergent. Teak oil is a waterproof finish which is suitable for most woods, but not lime. Apply as cooking oil. The rag used for applying teak oil should be burnt after use, as some types are liable to spontaneous combustion.

Boiled linseed oil usually darkens the wood, sometimes considerably over a period of several days as the oil hardens inside the wood. Numerous applications may be necessary before the wood begins to shine, although the finished result is well worth the effort, but not with pale timbers. With very hard timbers the oil needs to be diluted with an equal volume of white spirit. It is preferable if the work is warm as this will also aid penetration of the oil.

7 Restoration

The following notes and dates refer to English work made in the major southern cities. Country workmanship was rather backward in quality and style, and the materials used tended to be the local ones.

American and European carving and carved furniture do not necessarily bear any direct relationship with that of other countries. This is due to the different trading links and local materials, and the poor communications.

Ageing of timber
As timber ages it will normally darken. Oak can turn from pale brown to black, but this darkening with age is counteracted by the bleaching effect of sunlight. In strong sunlight, the bleaching will win, particularly with polished rosewood which can turn almost white. However, if you look at the bottom of the wood, or scratch the pale surface, it can be almost jet black. This is where it gets particularly difficult, for the bleaching is in the polish and the surface fibres of the wood, but the darkening penetrates much deeper. It is this subtle greyness which forms part of the patina and is almost impossible to reproduce with stains or chemicals.

The amount of darkening varies considerably with the timber and the polish on it. Ash will normally age to a soft brown, with an oil polish it can have a sickly yellowish tint as do several other very pale woods. Oak can age gradually to a rich brown, but rapidly with an oil polish. Shellac finishes will slow down the darkening of the wood under them, although the polish itself will change colour. Wax polishes in or on the wood will absorb dust. This produces what many people call the patina, but is actually just a surface layer of dirt.

Beetles and fungi
See also chapter 2, Preservation

Treatment with preservatives, woodworm killer or rot killer will reduce the adhesive properties of glue and appear to discolour the wood until the drying out process is complete. This can be a lengthy procedure, particularly with badly decayed wood which absorbs large amounts of fluid. Owing to this it is not normally feasible to apply the fluid until after the restoration and polishing have been completed. Where rot is present it is important to first remove the source of water.

The correct grade of Cuprinol can be liberally applied by either brush or spray to unpolished areas of the wood, particularly the end grain. Where there is polish over thick pieces of timber with woodworm it is necessary to inject the fluid through the worm holes. With thin timber it is generally possible to treat the back, and allow the fluid to soak through to the front of the wood. When rot is present the timber is normally able to absorb Cuprinol *Dry Rot Killer* like a sponge, the rot normally being present in un-polished areas of the base or back.

Seduction of woodworm

One difficulty of treating worm is that some fabrics and materials in contact with the wood may be adversely affected. An example is the canvas of an oil painting. In the rare instances where chemicals cannot be used, it is possible to entice the worm out. When the beetles lay their eggs at the end of the life cycle, they will do so on the most suitable timber. Favourites include European beech and walnut, but not American black walnut. The wood must be rough sawn and have plenty of splits, so providing ample crevices for the beetles to lay their eggs. Place this timber in the closest possible proximity to the piece of wood which you wish to rescue. Burn and replace the 'baits' at the end of every summer, after all the eggs have been laid.

Matching wood

Replacing a missing piece of carving means matching the species, age, colour, grain pattern, grain direction and medullary ray of the timber. The more of the above features which can be matched, the more invisible will be the repair. Unfortunately, the timbers are not always what they appear to be: the satinwood may be stained birch, ebony stained pear, rosewood stained walnut, and everything might be wood-filler.

The usual procedure is to cut the broken edge cleanly, preferably parallel to the grain direction. If the angle of the joint is very oblique to the grain, see the section headed 'Dowelling' below.

Surface colour of timber is invariably different from the wood below it. Consequently, the perfect repair is carried out with old matching timber and polish, and the replacement wood is so fitted that the layer of polish matches the polish around it. This is of course rarely possible except for flat areas and simple mouldings. The usual method is to take old timber from derelict houses or badly damaged furniture, and cut a block slightly larger than necessary to replace the missing piece.

After the wood has been glued into place, the surplus is then cut away.

Dowelling

Bodgers usually use screws, or at worst nails, to repair fractures and replace missing carving. Nails and screws often weaken the joint and certainly cause serious problems when later restoration is carried out. Enthusiastic amateurs may try to be too efficient and use metal dowels. Iron will cause serious discoloration in oak and some other timbers. In any wood, the moisture content will react with the iron to form rust, which will expand and eventually burst open the timber.

Wood expands and contracts with changes in the humidity, copper or brass dowels move with changes in temperature. In addition to this, furniture will flex as it is used, but a metal dowel

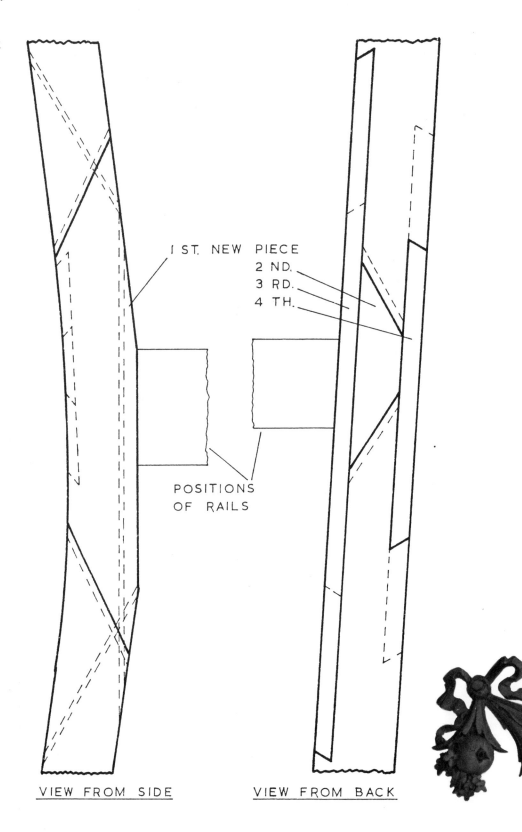

139 Splicing broken Chippendale chair back

I ST. NEW PIECE
2 ND.
3 RD.
4 TH.

POSITIONS OF RAILS

VIEW FROM SIDE

VIEW FROM BACK

will not. The result is that any glue joint between the wood and metal will soon fracture – despite claims of certain manufacturers. Apart from a metal dowel producing a weak joint, the stiffness of the metal will tend to make any subsequent breakage much more serious.

I recommend the use of wooden dowels made from a non-oily timber. A method of positioning these without any accurate surfaces to measure from, is to tap a small panel pin about 3mm ($\frac{1}{8}$in.) into one of the broken surfaces where a dowel is required. Cut the heads of the pins so that about 1·5mm ($\frac{1}{16}$in.) is above the wood. If the broken parts are accurately placed together, then the dowel centres will be marked on each.

Splicing

Chair backs have a habit of breaking straight across the grain at the junction of the back and seat frame. This point has not only the greatest stress, but also the greatest weakness caused by the carving and joints coinciding. Many decorative carvings will also break in the same way, when two heavy portions are joined by a weaker one. Designs of this type with motifs bunched together are quite common with work in the style of Grinling Gibbons (140). In cases like these it is often impossible to fit a heavy dowel without making the carving even more fragile.

The basic principles are to fit the new wood across the break with only the minimum amount of new wood showing and where it will provide the greatest strength. Any cuts made directly across the grain will have the greatest weakness and appear to be the most objectionable.

An efficient technique is to:

1   Glue the broken parts together using a scrap piece of wood as a splint.

2   With the splint still in position, mark out the first piece of wood to be cut away. Use a fine toothed tenon saw or dovetail saw to sever the fibres and remove the waste with a narrow bevel edge chisel.

3   Cut a piece of replacement wood (see Matching Wood, page 105) ensuring that all surfaces are perfectly flat.

4   Rub chalk onto the replacement wood, then rub this wood into the work.

140 Floral swag in the style of Grinling Gibbons
150mm × 710mm × 45mm
(6in. × 28in. × 1$\frac{3}{4}$in.)
By courtesy of R. Hunt

5   Highlights so marked where the chalk rubs off are then removed with the widest possible bevel edge chisel.
6   Continue steps 4 and 5 until all high spots are removed.
7   Glue will not stick to chalk, so this must be chiselled or planed off, without destroying any of the flat surfaces or angles.
8   Glue the first piece of wood into place before marking out and cutting any subsequent pieces.

An alternative to rubbing with chalk is to use water which can then be dried off. With very small repairs, simply rubbing the wood together will produce shiny highlights.

Distressing
Even if the colour and grain of replacement timber are perfectly matching, the effect will be disturbing if the new wood is in pristine condition. Distressing is the gentle art of copying wear, in the places where it would naturally occur. Smashing a good piece of carving with a length of chain is worse than doing nothing. Suitable tools are: Fine abrasive paper to wear sharp corners, chain, rubbed against the work, to wear the softer parts of the timber and leave the harder parts standing in ridges, rough broken concrete and unusual shaped pieces of stone, to create fine dents and scratches. In addition to physical wear, it is necessary to apply stains and chemicals – again in the places where they would naturally be spilt.

Making 'Woodworm holes'
One point which causes problems is the woodworm hole. The grub lives just below the surface of the wood and makes a neat round exit hole in the spring. Any simulated woodworm hole must therefore be drilled straight into the wood, but bend just below the surface. An easy method of detecting a fake woodworm hole is to push a small pin head into it – this being used to feel the depth and curvature of the hole. The most satisfactory method of making the woodworm hole is with a spherical dental drill. If a dental burr is not available, then a normal drill can be used but only a very shallow hole must be made. Holes must vary slightly in size and the groupings must be irregular, but concentrated in the sapwood (58).

Staining
Traditional staining was carried out with vegetable dye extracted from plants such as walnuts, tea or coffee. In addition, pigment such as blood could be added to the actual polish. Synthetic dyes are now used but many of these, like the original vegetable dyes, will fade in sunlight. Water based stains are least affected by light. They are also best in that the colour tends to be clear and brilliant, and an even colour is easy to obtain. Naptha stains tend to give a muddy colour, spirit stains will run quickly into the end grain, so giving excessive colour variations on shaped work. If a spirit stain must

be used, it is safer to apply a thin sealing coat of polish to the wood. The stain is then mixed in with a second coat of polish.

Water stains may be applied by sponge, brush or airbrush. For large, flat areas a sponge is efficient. Brushing directly onto the wood can cause colour differences where the brush marks overlap, unless the stain is applied in several thin coats. Eveness of colour can be further improved by damping the wood and applying the water stain to the moist timber.

When an old carving is closely inspected, the colour variations may be gradual, but are often quite extreme. It is the subtle graduation which is very difficult to achieve with a normal brush. In contrast, an airbrush can provide extremely subtle or sharp contrasts. Apply the colours as they would be in the original carving:

1   Original colour of timber evenly applied to all the new work.
2   Correct any variations of figuring.
3   Add the darkening caused by age, but particularly on the areas which would receive the least light.
4   Bleaching effect on areas receiving the most light.
5   Dust on upper areas.
6   Polish – thinly applied where it would wear off, more thickly in hollows where you would expect it to collect.
7   Dirty wax polish thinly applied on extreme highlights, very thickly around the highlights but almost none in the hollows.

See *Finishing*, page 101 and *A summary of period styles and techniques*, page 111, for an introduction to the finishing process. The actual techniques are variable – every polisher will recommend something different, and every description needs a complete volume. See Appendix, page 118, Suppliers of books.

Timbers in restoration

The following timbers are almost exclusively met with in restoration.

Birch mahogany, mahogany birch, mountain mahogany or sweet birch Birch has been used throughout Europe and America but birch mahogany is the species reserved for the finer work. Formerly imported from Quebec.

Coramandel   A form of ebony having a ground colour variable between light and dark brown, figured with black stripes and marks. Logs seldom have a diameter above 230mm (9in.).

Mahogany, African 480–610 30–38   Large quantities were imported in the early 1830s. It very rapidly fell into extreme disfavour and was little used until the twentieth century. The scarcity of better timber forces it to be used for reproduction work.

Mahogany, Cuban 640 40   Imported from the West Indies and used extensively, particularly during the second half of the eighteenth and during the nineteenth centuries for furniture and carving. The colour is a rich dark reddish brown, often with white deposits in the pores. Grain is interlocked but often with very rich figuring. The wood is brittle but stable and with a harder and finer texture than the African and Honduras mahoganies (63).

Mahogany, Honduras 545 34   A Central American mahogany which is lighter and softer than Cuban. It is however the same species as Cuban but grown on different soils. Colour varies from a pale golden to a rich dark colour almost indistinguishable from Cuban. Grain is however straighter and less interlocked. Stable. Used from the late eighteenth century. This wood is much lighter in weight than the Cuban or Spanish varieties. It is thus possible to date a piece of work, simply by feeling the weight.

Mahogany, Spanish, Jamaican or San Domingo   This is the finest of the mahoganies and was the first mahogany to become popular in the eighteenth century, and being the most popular until the middle of the century. It has a richer and more mellow appearance than Cuban or Honduras. Close grained, firm and heavy but with little figure.

Oak 720 45   Oak ages from an off white to a rich dark brown. Old oak is almost commonly available in the form of beams taken from demolition sites, gate posts or damaged furniture. Even if old timber is not available it is possible to use brown oak. Brown oak is not a distinct species, but has been subject to a slow form of decay during the growth of the tree. The brown colour so formed can be used to blend in with very much older timber (32).

Bog oak is the common oak which has been buried in a bog, the colour often changing to jet black. Commonly used as decorative veneer in cabinet work, but very prone to shakes when used in the solid. An early method of trying to prevent this was to rub size, or weak glue into the pores of the wood. Since Victorian times blackened plaster of Paris was also used, prior to french polishing.

Rosewood, Rio 865 54   Rio rosewood was the best species used from the late eighteenth century and through most of the nineteenth century. Comparatively inferior Indian rosewood was then used to some extent, but the South American variety was used for quality work. It is now extremely expensive and almost unobtainable. Colouring and figuring in this timber are much superior to other rosewoods, markings being almost black and the ground a clear rich red. It is unsuitable for detailed work but was extensively used for this during the nineteenth century.

Do not use an oil polish, but sealing and waxing is very effective. Victorians filled the pores of the wood with coloured plaster of Paris, papered it off and then used french polish (66).

Satinwood 995 62   Imported during the late eighteenth, nineteenth and early twentieth centuries from the East and West Indies. Satinwood is related to mahogany and has a close grain of a pale yellow colour. The hard interlocked wood has a distinctive figuring and silky lustre. When french polished, as in Victorian work, satinwood retains its yellow colour. In contrast, Georgian work was often polished with beeswax and the yellow colour was rapidly lost, leaving a pale blanched appearance. Early work has often been subsequently stained and re-polished to a golden brown (1).

See 'Timbers', Chapter 2, for other woods which are still in common use.

A summary of period styles and techniques

Jacobean 1603–1649

Oak was used almost entirely, but also some pine, pear and lime. Carving was usually either incised or low relief, with the background lowered to leave the highest areas level with the panel surface. Popular motifs were the guilloche, elaborate or flowered half circles, tulip, acanthus, vines, channeling, foliated and floral scrolls.

Wood was often unfinished or waxed, but the most popular finish was oil and wax. Nut or poppy oil was used, this being rubbed into the work and surplus wiped off. (The nearest commonly available modern equivalent is boiled linseed oil.) After drying, the surface was then waxed with pure beeswax. Inferior woods were generally painted black. Coloured paints were also used on the better work in oak.

See page 103 for notes on how to make beeswax polish.

141 Chip carved chest 1648 Victoria and Albert Museum, London

Cromwellian 1649–1660
Oak was still the most popular material and the Jacobean period had some influence on the style of carving. However, the Puritan spirit restrained all forms of decoration, making carving very rare.

The finishes used were the same as during the Jacobean period.

Carolean 1660–1688 (36)
Walnut was the material which began to supercede oak. With walnut came the fashion for carving 'twist-turned' legs. (See chapter 5, 'Turning' and 'Twist Turning'.)

Grinling Gibbons, working mainly in lime, set an elaborate style. Very low relief carving was often replaced with three dimensional work and the style became much more exuberant (94). The Flemish scroll was popularized, the introduction of caning affected chair design and double doors closing together affected cabinet design. Much of the change was due to the Huguenots who started to flee from France and its colonies in 1680.

Finishing was similar to that used during the Jacobean period, but painting and gilding were much more fashionable.

William and Mary 1689–1702
Oak and local timbers were used for country work. Finer work was in walnut, but pine, pear and lime were used when the final finish was to be gilt. Elaborate styles were used, mainly in high relief and three dimensional work. Upholstery, introduced a century before, now became fashionable. Swags, figures, flowers, acanthus, cockles, Flemish scrolls and other motifs were used (140).

Shellac was introduced as a finish for marquetry, but carving and plain furniture may have been oiled, waxed, painted or gilded.

Queen Anne 1702–1714
Walnut was still the fashionable timber with other materials such as beech being coloured to simulate it. Pine, pear and lime were used when the finish was to be gilt or lacquer. Local timbers were also used for country work. Cabriole legs took their basic shape from animal legs when introduced from France. Apart from the basic shaping, these had carved decoration and often ended with a hoof. Carving was much more refined than during the William and Mary period.

Finishes were oil, wax, shellac, paint, lacquer and gilt. Gilding was often used to highlight ornate carving, surrounding areas of plain wood being polished. Oak was usually oiled and waxed while shellac was more popular for walnut.

George 1 1714–1727
Very similar to Queen Anne but walnut started to decline. Ball and claw feet and later mahogany became fashionable. Mahogany was usually finished with shellac, but sometimes oiled and waxed.

George II 1727–1760
Walnut rapidly fell into disfavour and was replaced with mahogany.

Queen Anne styles were refined, elaborated and embellished in a bold and vigorous style, often with a French influence. Bird and animal forms were extensively used, along with masks, scrolls, foliage and classical designs. Softwoods were used in conjunction with gilt, but mahogany to be finely carved was generally polished with shellac.

Adam 1728–1792
Robert Adam inspired a classical revival in the sixties. Satinwood increased in popularity from 1770 until the end of the century. Many exotic woods were also used but Mahogany was always the most fashionable.

Much of the fine detail was in fact cast with materials such as glue and plaster and depicted delicate classical motifs – the overall effect being elegant and architectural.

Chippendale 1718–1779
Thomas Chippendale's *Gentleman and Cabinet Maker's Director* first appeared in 1754. He applied the rococo style of decoration in a less excessive form. He also used the Chinese and Gothic influences. Chippendale's English style comprised lion's heads (142), human and grotesque masks carved onto knees of chairs and table underframes. Also ball and claw feet, acanthus and egg and dart mouldings.

142 Lion's head. Late Chippendale period. Pine
230mm × 280mm × 150mm
(9in. × 11in. × 6in.)
Gilt

Hepplewhite

George Hepplewhite's claim to fame was *The Cabinet Maker and Upholsterer's Guide*, which first appeared in 1788, two years after his death. His work was delicately shaped and carved, with more curves and flowing lines than Adam (1). Notable is the shield back on chairs, often carved with the Prince of Wales feathers.

Sheraton 1751–1806

Thomas Sheraton produced *The Cabinet-maker and Upholsterer's Drawing-book*, the first edition of which appeared in 1791. His furniture is light and delicate, bridging the gap between neo-classical and Regency. Dark mahogany was the wood normally carved, being decorated with reeding, fluting and low reliefs of acanthus, floral wreaths, leaves, flowers, etc.

Finishing during the second half of the eighteenth century was variable. Earlier work may have been oiled and waxed. Sealing with thin coats of shellac dissolved in alcohol, and a final coat of beeswax dissolved in turpentine was more common, particularly where painted decoration was sealed on (1).

A popular finish on chairs and other highly ornate work was simply wax. There were also several variations of oiling and waxing. One method was to grind up a brick. The final finish was then obtained by sifting the brick through a fine bag onto the waxed surface before buffing. Eighteenth century bricks produced a fine red dust which filled the pores, giving a better polish with the final rubbing. Another variation was to apply linseed oil. This was allowed to stand for two days on softwood, but seven on hardwood. Brick dust was also sifted thickly onto this before vigorous rubbing. Surplus oil was then removed with bran of wheat flour. Owing to the friction required, this method could only be used on plain or moulded surfaces.

Regency 1800–1830

Mahogany and rosewood were the most fashionable woods, being carved into classical motifs such as the honeysuckle and ionic columns. Designs were rather restrained and the only carving on furniture was often restricted to mouldings.

Previously mentioned methods of finishing were used, but towards the end of this period, french polishing became fashionable. Varnish was often used as a base coat, to quickly build up a thick layer of polish. Oak used for country furniture could be fumed by hanging it in a stable, the fumes darkening the wood. The modern method is to seal the furniture in a box with a saucer of ammonia.

Appendix

Abrasives – a table of comparative coarseness

Steel wool is numbered grade 3 (very coarse), 2, 1, 0, 00, 000 and 0000 (very fine). Regrettably, the abrasiveness varies from one manufacturer to another – sometimes there is even considerable variation within a packet.

Abrasive papers which are of use to the woodcarver are aluminium oxide, garnet, glasspaper and silicon carbide. Following is a comparison of the three different numbering systems in common use:

—	—	600
—	—	500
—	10/0	400
—	9/0	360
—	—	320
—	8/0	280
—	7/0	240
—	6/0	220
00	5/0	180
0	4/0	150
1	3/0	120
1½	2/0	100
F2	0	80
M2	½	60
S2	1	50
2½	1½	40
3	2	36
—	2½	30
—	3	24
—	3½	20
—	4	16
—	4½	12

Copyright

These notes are only intended as a layman's guide. Further details may be obtained from The Copyright Act 1956, or a solicitor.

An original piece of work has two things of value to the sculptor – the copyright and the sculpture itself. These two things can be sold separately, for the sale of the original work of art does not in any way dispose of the copyright.

A piece of sculpture is published when it is displayed for sale or hire. Exhibition in any form is not regarded as publication. If the work is never published then the copyright lasts for ever. If the publication takes place, then the copyright continues for fifty years after the death of the sculptor, calculated from the end of the calender year in which he or she dies.

The sculptor owns the copyright in any work which he creates, in any work created by an apprentice to the sculptor and in any photographs of the work commissioned by the sculptor.

Reproductions for the purposes of criticism, review and education are permissible. Also, if a work is sited in a public place, people may photograph, draw or paint it.

Protection is given to the form, but not the idea, so that there is no infringement if the idea is copied in a different form. The owner of the copyright can take legal proceedings against anyone who knowingly persists in breaking the copyright, either by selling, hiring, exhibiting for sale or hire or by importing any unauthorised reproduction of the work into the United Kingdom. A reproduction includes three dimensional copies and two dimensional copies, such as paintings and photographs.

Copyright can be disposed of by a simple signed letter. Granting a licence is more businesslike; the copyright then remains the sculptors, but there is an agreement not to enforce your rights against the licencee. Have the contract legally drawn up, limiting the number of reproductions and the length of time that the licence is to run.

When a piece of sculpture is to be used as a design for mass reproduction it is exempt from The Copyright Act. Instead, it comes under the Registered Designs Act, 1949. Consult a solicitor or patent agent about having it registered.

Laws throughout the western world do vary to some degree, they are however basically similar to those in force in the United Kingdom.

Courses

Local evening classes
Council for Small Industries in Rural Areas
35 Camp Road
London SW19
Tel. 01-946 5101
West Dean College
West Dean
Chichester
Sussex
Tel Singleton 301

Residential Short Courses
A half yearly directory of courses in England and Wales
Published by the National Institute of Adult Education, 35 Queen Anne Street, London W1

Vacation Courses Abroad
Published by the Central Bureau for Educational Visits and Exchanges, 43 Dorset Street, London W1
Tel 01-486 5101

Craft societies and associations

Art Information Registry (AIR)
Burlington House
Piccadilly, London W1
Tel 01-734 3604

Royal Society of British Sculptors
108 Old Brompton Road
South Kensington
London SW7 3RA
Tel 01-373 5554

Society of Designer-Craftsmen
6 Queen Square
London WC1N 3AR
Tel 01-328 4397

The Guild of Master Craftsmen
10 Dover Street
London W1X 3PH
Tel 01-493 7571/2

A complete list of craft societies, including regional ones, is available from:

Crafts Advisory Committee
12 Waterloo Place
London SW1Y 4AU
Tel 01-839 1917

Estimating
The number of people who will appreciate your work is inversely proportional to the quality of your products. This is further complicated by the fact that I only once met a truly honest dealer – he went bankrupt.

I calculate the price for a given job and come as close to it as possible. When I meet somebody who seems to be in the habit of quibbling the price goes up by 20 per cent, in order to let them have their 10 per cent discount. Whatever happens, try not to cut the quality, its always tempting but one small compromise leads to another.

This will soon give you an excellent reputation as a bodger, and a guarantee not to have another job of any quality.

Overheads include all general expenses which cannot be charged to any particular work:
Accountant
Advertising
Bank charges
Car depreciation (capital allowance)
Car parking and garaging
Car, general running
Electricity
Gas
Insurance
Machines, depreciation
National insurance contributions
Postage
Property maintenance
Protective clothing
Public transport
Rates
Rent
Society fees
Stationery
Telephone
Tools, etc.

Even if you own your workshop you should still charge a theoretical rent, to compensate for lack of income from your bank manager. The total list of overheads is added up and divided by the theoretical number of working hours in a year, after allowing for sickness, holidays and paperwork. This answer is added to the hourly wage necessary to give a reasonable standard of living – annoyingly, this usually comes to very much less than a plumber or garage mechanic will charge.

Calculating the time necessary to do a given job is a matter of practice. Start by keeping a file with a card for every job which you do. Count every minute spent on a job, breaking it down into designing, collection and delivery, carving and polishing. To this add expenses such as wood, sub-contracting of preliminary machining and gilding. The same file card also notes the price quoted on a job, the percentages added to sub-contractors fees, expenses and when payment was made – very handy for calculating how much you owe the tax man.

Estimating for restoration work is particularly difficult. That innocent looking coat of thick black varnish which you have just estimated will take 20 hours to remove, may be there to hide another 50 hours of work: nails, screws, metal plates, wood filler, new timber of the incorrect species with the grain running in the wrong direction and other examples of common business practice. Also, when a Chippendale mirror frame has a piece missing from one side, the corresponding piece on the other side may be broken off, so making the original fault less noticeable. This last example is a true one, carried out by one of London's leading department stores!

Information

Technical, managerial and financial support for rural craftsmen in England and Wales is available from:

Council for Small Industries in Rural Areas
(CoSIRA)
35 Camp Road
London SW19

The Scottish equivalent of CoSIRA is:

Small Industries Council for Rural Areas of Scotland
(SICRAS)
27 Walker Street
Edinburgh

Financial support and general information is available from:

Crafts Advisory Committee (CAC)
12 Waterloo Place
London SW1Y 4AU

The Small Firms Information Service is backed by the Department of Industry. It has a series of centres which can provide all forms of free information:

57 Bothwell Street
Glasgow G2 6TU

16 St David's House
Wood Street
Cardiff CF1 1ER

22 Newgate Shopping Centre
Newcastle upon Tyne NE1 5RH

Peter House
Oxford Street
Manchester M1 5AN

5 Royal Exchange House
City Square
Leeds LS1 5PQ

48–50 Maid Marian Way
Nottingham NG1 6GF

53 Stephenson Street
Birmingham B2 4DH

35 Wellington Street
Luton LU1 2SB

65 Buckingham Palace Road
London SW1W 0QX

Colston Centre
Colston Avenue
Bristol BS1 4UB

A similar service is provided in Northern Ireland by the Department of Commerce.

An independent research organisation which provides information about wood is:

Timber Research and Development Association
(TRADA)
Hughenden Valley
High Wycombe
Buckinghamshire HP14 4ND

Publicity

1 Design and print a distinctive letterhead on quality paper.
2 Have business cards to match.
3 Find a good professional photographer and commission him to take large glossy photographs of your work. Use these to show prospective patrons, give to the press or use in exhibitions.
4 Some of the photographs can be used to print Christmas cards, post cards and notelets, very cheap forms of publicity. Try to persuade shop keepers, particularly local ones, to sell them for you. Give boxes of notelets as Christmas presents.
5 Notify the press whenever you complete a major commission.
6 Make sure that your signature on work is prominent and legible.

Suppliers

Adhesives
Aerolite and *Araldite* are available from most hardware shops. Technical advice may be obtained from:

Ciba-Geigy
Duxford, Cambridgeshire

Animal glue is available by mail order from:

Fiddes and Son
Trade Street
Cardiff

Woodcraft Supply Corporation
313 Montvale Avenue
Woburn
Massachusetts 01801

Evo-Stik is available from most hardware shops. Technical advice may be obtained from:

Evode Ltd
Common Road
Stafford ST16 3EH

Books
Specialist technical books are available by mail order from:

Stobart and Son Ltd
67/73 Worship Street
London EC2A 2EL

Woodcraft Supply Corporation
313 Montvale Avenue
Woburn Massachusetts 01801

Crossbow components
A mail order firm which supplies technical advice and everything from detailed working drawings to telescopic sights for night use is:

B. and P. Barnett
Unit 4
Ettingshall Industrial Estate
Ettingshall Road
Wolverhampton
Shropshire

Preservatives
Preservatives, woodworm and rot killers are widely available from builders merchants. Technical advice may be obtained from:

Cuprinol Ltd
Customer Advisory Service
Adderwell, Frome
Somerset BA11 1NL

Spray finishing equipment
A list of retail outlets and technical advice about Airbrushes and other finishing equipment is available from:

The DeVilbiss Co. Ltd
Ringwood Road
Bournemouth BH11 9LH

Tools
Record Ridgway Tools Ltd
Parkway Works
Sheffield S9 3BL

This group of companies produces nearly all the tools suitable for the woodcarver, including many unusual tools which are very difficult to find elsewhere; examples are the Circular Plane (020C), Drawknife (M1160) and Inside Ground Paring Gouge with cranked neck. These tools are available through normal tool shops, but write or phone the above address in case of difficulty, or for technical advice.

Woodcarving tools are available by mail order from:

Alec Tiranti Ltd
21 Goodge Place
London W1

Woodcraft Supply Corporation
313 Montvale Avenue
Woburn, Massachusetts 01801

Wood
A mail order firm supplying European and exotic timbers, which can be delivered anywhere in the country is:

North Heigham Sawmills
Paddock Street
Norwich NR2 4TW

Wood finishes
A mail order firm which supplies a wide variety of polishes, abrasives, stains, gold leaf and other materials for wood finishing is:

Fiddes and Son
Trade Street
Cardiff

Index